Gold and Silver Profits:
How To Build Wealth and Safely Invest In Gold and Silver

Anthony T. Mellinger

Library House Books
www.libraryhousebooks.com
Paramount, CA.

Copyright 2018

All rights reserved. No part of this book may be reproduced in any format or by any means without written permission from the publisher.

Library of Congress Cataloging-in-Publication
Available at Worldcat

Gold and Silver Profits:
How To Build Wealth and Safely Invest In Gold and Silver
Anthony T. Mellinger

ISBN: 978-1-936828-62-3 (Softcover)

TABLE OF CONTENTS

Introduction 2
Inflation 3
E-Gold 31
Goldmoney 33
Electronic Gold and Silver 35
Other Ways to Invest 36
Internet Auction Site Scams 39
Tips From The American Numismatic Association: 43
Resource Articles 44
Helpful Reference Materials 46
Investing in Gold? What's the Rush? 48
Investing In Bullion and Bullion Coins 52
Glossary of Gold 56
Investing in Collectible Coins 57
The Gold Report Interview 65
Why Buy Gold 81
Buying Gold 87
Trust Issues in Buying Gold Coins 89
Gold, and How to Avoid the Scams in the Coin Industry 91
Index 139

INTRODUCTION

Against a backdrop of central banks selling their gold reserves, most notably the United Kingdom, which sold over half of the countries' gold reserves, 400 tonnes, at the almost rock bottom average price of $270 per ounce between 1999 and 2002, Gold has risen from an absolute low of $250 to the current price of $1,746 in 2011. Silver has risen from under $5 to $40 over the same period. Investors are starting to notice and are wondering why these prices are rising and how they can invest. As you're reading this then you are probably interested, or are at least curious about investing in the precious metals of Gold and Silver. This book is an investigation into the reasons why you should consider including, most certainly, Gold and probably also Silver in your investment portfolio, followed by coverage of the many ways to do so, some of which you will have heard of and others you might not. The good news for most investors is that this book is intended for beginners. It will not dazzle you with pages of complex charts and options or derivatives trading methods, nor do you need to be an expert in mining companies and techniques, so one or more of the ways suggested will probably suit your style of investing.

Please note that where the book mentions actual fee costs or percentages for certain services, you should double check, as these often change with provider promotions and fee structure changes. The links to all sites mentioned in this publication are available at http:,,www.investgold.co.uk, and you can visit the links yourself to ascertain the current fees as part of calculating which investments will work best for you. And now for the legal bit, this book is not directly inducing you to invest or not invest in any particular product, merely to identify opportunities to invest more cheaply, so that more of your money remains your own and secondly to identify possible areas of precious metals in-vestment that are unknown to the majority of investors yet offer great scope to diversify your portfolio and improve your returns.

I hope you find the information contained within useful, stimulating and most of all PROFITABLE.

INFLATION

The Hidden Tax on Your Savings

You have probably never heard inflation called a tax be-fore, but in the opinion of many experts that is exactly what is. To appreciate this you have to understand that no matter where you are living as you read this, your currency today is not backed by anything more than the "full faith of the government", otherwise known as a Fiat currency. As the government controls this currency, they have to ability to turn off and on the taps in creation of this currency, which they do in the main by setting Interest Rates, but scarily they could always just resort to cranking up the printing presses to pay off their debts, although this is an extreme situation. Assuming the setting of interest rates tool is used, a low interest rate stimulates the economy by encouraging more people to borrow more money and thus more money is issued by the lending bank, while a high interest rate discourages more borrowing and forces repayment of existing debt. In case you are not quite clear, the last paragraph mentions the lending bank is issuing money. This means that subject to certain requirements, a lending bank is allowed to create money out of thin air when loaning money. It is a popular misconception that there has to be an equivalent deposit in the bank made by someone else. This is known as fractional reserve banking. Under this system, a bank is allowed to create loans for multiples of the deposits it holds. For example, consider a scenario where a bank has to retain only 20% of its deposits as a reserve. If you deposit £1,000 with a bank, then the bank may ultimately be allowed to loan out, say, £4,000 to potential borrowers. This means that there is extra £4,000 circulating in the economy, and that while you thought you were rich with your hard-earned £1,000, there are now other people with the exact same spending power as you, the only difference being that they produced that money via their own assumed future earnings. This is due to the cycle whereby borrowers spend their money on goods and services and the people receiving the money then deposit their new wealth in turn at a bank, who can then create even more loans against these new deposits. Now your original £1,000 deposit is being gradually diluted and it's spending power devalued by newly created currency. Something you probably do realize about inflation is that it means increases in the cost of the everyday items you need in order to live, but the real thing most people fail to realize is that these increases are often decreases in the value of your currency, usually due to the new currency creation schemes outlined. Your savings therefore should at least match the increase in inflation as of course the idea is that you will be able to cash them in at some point in future and enjoy at least the same benefit in spending them as you would from spending them right now. When it comes to the official government inflation figures, these often understate true increases in the cost of living, due to the statistical reporting methods used. As the famous old adage goes, there are "lies, damned lies and statistics", and nowhere could this be truer than here. One method is to reduce the real price still further if the assumed quality of an item included in the basket of goods has gone up in quality.

For example, a 2007 computer could be classified as ten times more powerful than a 1997 computer, and even though they have the same retail price of say, £1,000; the figures are adjusted downward due to the increased processing power: whether you really needed that extra processing power, or whether it is even possible to buy a 1997 specification computer is not considered. Another method is replacement, or substitution theory, where as a hypothetical example, say, if high quality beef rises in price, then it is assumed that many households will trade down to cheaper beef, or even some other type of meat.

Whether or not these are correct ways to measure price increases in anything is open to conjecture, but they do ultimately have the effect of making the official inflation figures lower. Once upon a time, right up to the 1920s, most currencies were backed by gold, and you could walk into, say, the Bank of England and exchange your pound notes for the equivalent gold amount stated on them. These must have been happier times in many ways, since the value of your currency was fixed and the price of goods remained stable. This of course meant that your savings were virtually guaranteed to buy you a similar standard of living in the future as they would today.

For cash savings, low interest rates are of course bad news, but falsely low rates as controlled by a government maybe trying to win popularity with voters before an election rather than managing rates correctly, are bad news in another, more insidious way in that they cause more inflation and thus devalue your existing savings more rapidly. As a share investor, inflation can lead to large rises in the profits stated by businesses, and at face value the obvious thing is to believe this is a good thing - in fact a dose of inflation is often presented as a good thing by governments. However, when businesses need to start working on recruiting new employees or buying new stock, they find that the prices for these items have started rising and their increased profitability was but a temporary phenomenon. In the worst cases, the raw materials to manufacture their product might actually now cost more than the price of their finished product and they could be driven out of business. At the worst extremes, and historically this has happened many hundreds of times, a government destroys it's currency by inflation. Eventually, the holders of Pounds (Great Britain 1931), Marks (Germany 1921-23), Livres (France 1790s), or whatever all realize that their currency is being devalued and endeavor to get rid of it as quick as possible by buying whatever they think will hold its value instead.

This has the effect of making the currency even more undesirable and worthless, which then becomes a downward spiral of which Zimbabwe is today's prime example. A lesser documented effect of the inflation in Zimbabwe has been that the Zimbabwean stock market has in fact risen well in excess of the corresponding inflation, as holders of Zimbabwean dollars try to exchange their worthless currency for something of value such as shares in reliable businesses, often with safe overseas earnings or hard assets such as property or mining rights.

The conclusion to draw from this is that in times of high inflation there are assets or businesses with pricing power that can protect you against the ravages of inflation. The complex issue of inflation comes back to but one simple consideration for the astute investor to think about; Diversification. You probably already have some cash savings, and that is no bad thing since you will always have expenses to meet in your home country and are not so exposed to a stock market crash, plus if a government is honest about an inflation situation and raises interest rates dramatically then your savings have the benefit of receiving dramatic interest rates. But to be truly diversified and protected, you definitely should be holding some of your savings in the one item in world history which has always retained its purchasing power, and has always been viewed as a tradable item for goods and services, and that is gold.

GOLD AND SILVER AS MONEY

This book does not intend to go into great detail on this subject, as many, many pages have been written by true experts through the ages. Furthermore there are just too many historical examples of unsoundly managed fiat currency destroying the savings of ordinary people to cover here, not that your government really wants you to ever know about this. A Reading List is available at http:,,www.investgold.co.uk, so what follows is just a brief outline. Gold (and silver) are traditionally the real units of currency upon which world trade is based. Historically they replaced all other forms of currency in civilization such as seashells, stones, crops, etc. that were used as items for trade and barter because they are durable and not easy to replicate, so their future value is relatively assured. Gold especially has a reputation for not tarnishing or rusting, and is even resistant to some strong acids, meaning that as far as a medium of exchange goes there is nothing, quite literally, "as good as gold". Paper money only came into being in the first place as a substitute for the practice of using physical gold and silver in transactions. What happened was that people de-posited their gold with a bank, and then the bank would issue them with a promissory note, or notes for the value of their gold. People could then use their notes to buy goods and the person receiving the note knew they now owned the amount of precious metal stated on the note. The real problems started occurring when people (normally banks, governments and forgers) began issuing extra notes backed by the same amount of precious metal, and, in 1971, the last historic link between gold and worldwide currency was removed by the USA, when they removed the link that 1 ounce of gold could be exchanged for 35 dollars and vice-versa. Up to this time, gold had a fixed value in terms of world trade. It seems to be that every great nation in history begins with good intentions of a strong currency, since prior to the USA, Britain removed it's link to gold in the 1920s, after its own inflation problems due to the costs of paying for World War 1. The USA removed its link, at least in part, due to the cost of paying for the Vietnam War. During the 1960s, prior to removing the gold peg, they had built up to this by also removing from circulation all lower priced silver coinage, such as dimes and nickels, and minting new, cheaper alloy versions with the same face value. Coincidentally (although perhaps not), the 1970s then saw rampant inflation, with gold finally reaching an all-time high of $850 dollars per ounce in 1980 and Silver peaking at $49 in 1980 after beginning the decade at un-der $2. Yes, you read that right, a 20-times plus return for holding what are probably the world's safest stores of value in your pocket. Could such times be repeated? Well, tie in today's current period of government-reported low inflation figures and indifference amongst a general population that has forgotten that gold and silver used to be the coins in our pockets to the mounting costs of wars in Afghanistan and Iraq. Sounds eerily similar, and therefore you might want to exchange some of your paper money "backed by the full faith of the Government" for some Gold, just in case. The book "Empire of Debt" is an interesting read in this respect. It cannot be guaranteed that your Gold investments will increase 20-fold in terms of your local currency, but it is guaranteed, barring theft (governmental or otherwise) or such like that your ounce of gold will still be worth an ounce of gold, less any fees, when you choose to cash it in, and that it will still be tradable for an ounce of gold worth of goods such as food and clothing. This applies even if the Government goes bankrupt and the Dollar or Pound ever becomes a worthless piece of paper. Just remember that whereas a government can print off as much currency as it likes, the amount of gold and silver can only increase by the amount that is mined yearly less the amount that is lost to manufacturing. In a bad year there could actually be less of this commodity in circulation than the previous year! This is especially true of silver, which in addition to its wealth value has a large number of manufacturing uses, such as in photography and electronics that deplete stocks. It is also worth noting here that Gold is a purer representative of true wealth than silver. Although both metals have been heavily used throughout history as currency and to represent wealth. Gold has few uses apart from as money, whereas Silver is a heavily used industrial commodity and that can affect its price and desirability out-side of any investment considerations. For example, some commentators are convinced that the rise of digital photography and the resultant downturn in traditional photography will result in a massive decrease in demand for silver, affecting the price as a result. This may or may not turn out to be true. Apparently, the US government issues each of its pilots with 2 gold sovereigns to use for trade if they are ever shot down in enemy territory. Note that they don't issue them with a huge wad of paper dollars, which probably says something about the worldwide appeal of gold as a tradable item over even the most well-known internationally accepted national currency. A more recent historical story of proof of Gold's real value came in 1933 at the height of the US depression. At this time an ounce of gold was exchangeable for $20 by government decree, but then the government made ownership of Gold illegal for US citizens and ordered the forcible confiscation of all privately held gold. After-wards gold was revalued to $35 an ounce, although it remained illegal for a US citizen to own Gold right up until the 1970s. As you can probably see, if as a US citizen you held gold at this time you just got robbed of $15 for each ounce you originally held! The other side of the equation was that there were suddenly 75% more dollars in circulation, backed by the exact same underlying amount of gold. Possible Government confiscation is also something you might want to consider when choosing your investments and, as we'll see later, there are many new ways to hold your gold that were simply not possible for ordinary citizens all those years ago.

The US governments example from 1933 is merely an-other example of debasing the coinage, a practice that existed as far back as Roman times, and probably before that. In this scheme, if a coin was originally 90% gold, and the government needed some more coins in circulation, then they would re-melt the same coins as 80% gold, with the rest of copper or such like. This meant that they could then generate an extra number of coins to spend on their own schemes, such as costly foreign wars. Ultimately of course, the price of goods rose to reflect the debased coinage. Note that to prevent citizens from de-basing the coinage by clipping the edges off themselves, coins often have a ribbed rim around the edge - a practice that continues to this day on many coins, gold or otherwise.

By now, you hopefully understand the difference between currency by governmental decree and hard currency. You may or may not also have realized that in reality. Gold, as the world's oldest currency, is the item of constant value, and that it is national currencies which decline or fall in value compared to the price of Gold. When you start looking at things this way, you begin to realize that when commentators talk about "the price of gold", this is a misnomer and perhaps a truer title would be "the value of the national currency", or such like.

Furthermore, when you link this fact with the chapter on Inflation, you begin to realize that another advantage of inflation for governments is that they are able to collect Capital Gains Taxes on illusory profits made by investors. As an example, if a national currency falls in value, by, say half, over a period of time and the value of your in-vestment doubles in that same time then it might look good on paper, but the reality is no more than the financial equivalent of standing still.

GOLD CONSPIRACIES

Following on from the previous two chapters you have probably derived certain conclusions about the vested interests of various parties in keeping the price of gold and silver low in relation to national currencies or conversely to make the value of national currencies not backed by anything, appear to be of some value. But in the words of Francis Urquhart, fictional UK Prime Minister in the top BBC Drama, "House of Cards";

"....you might think that, but I couldn't possibly comment". However coincidentally enough, the UK itself was home to a curious happening worthy of note in the field of Gold, when in 1999 it was decided to sell off over half the nations' gold reserves some 400 tonnes. At the time, Gold was at the end of a major 20-year bear market, and the price was at an all-time low, a price last seen in the 1970s. The Bank of England, custodian of the countries' Gold reserves insists that it was never consulted in the decision, and some leaks in fact suggest that many of their staff vigorously opposed the move. They claim that the decision was made by Her Majesty's Treasury, and them alone. At the time, the Chancellor of the Exchequer was a Mr. Gordon "Golden" Brown, who has subsequently become Prime Minister.

Gold Conspiracies

Even worse, the huge Gold sales and auctions were publicly announced well in advance thus giving gold deal-ers the chance to prepare for the glut of gold that was about to be released onto the market, and force the price down still further as a result. Normal strategy is to keep intended government gold sales quiet, then simply con-duct the sales on the open market, obtaining the best prices possible, then announce the results afterwards.

Why might a government decide to sell off one of the main assets of its people at the lowest price possible? Well, you might be surprised to hear that there are various Gold conspiracists, many of them persons of note in the financial world, who earnestly believe that the price of gold versus national currencies is often managed in this way and who have a field day with this sort of thing. In this case, there are rumors and accusations that the gold was sold to prevent top Hedge Funds who had gambled on the price of Gold from going bust and destroying the worldwide economy, among others.

This is just one story of many that the Gold conspiracists believe is occurring in our worldwide economy, and that, one day, people may realize, like Germans did in 1921-23, that their money is "not worth the paper it's printed on". This book has no specific comment to make on any aspect of this case, except that 1999-2002 has subsequently been proved to have been exactly the right time to start buying Gold, not selling it; in fact, the value of the Gold sold by the UK has risen by over five billion dollars since that time. If you want to know more about this story, and other alleged conspiracy theories behind

Gold, then please visit the web home of the Gold Anti-Trust action committee (GATA) a well-known organization, who believe that the value of Gold is being secretly manipulated.

Another major concern of note for GATA is the fact that of the Gold reserves still held by major nations, much of it has been loaned out. In this case, the custodians of the gold, the central banks loan out their gold to a third party, who pays an agreed interest for loan of the gold. This third party can then do whatever they like with the gold, including selling it on. This is a likely deal if the borrower wanted to gamble on the price of Gold falling, for example. The original agreement is, of course, that an equivalent amount of gold will one day be returned to the central bank.

But no audits have ever been carried out to find out how much physical Gold the central banks really hold, and how much has been loaned out. If there was ever a major crisis and the central banks want their Gold back, what is the likelihood that all of it will be returned, or be available to be returned by the borrowing parties? And what will be the effect on the price of Gold if these borrowers are forced to all at once buy fresh Gold to honor their promises? For example, the USA remains the nation that reports the largest Gold reserves in the world, but in the absence of concrete evidence, many commentators are dubious how much Gold the USA still really has in safe-keeping.

Silver is not without its own conspiracy theories. As a much used industrial commodity, it is in the best interests of many to keep the price as low as possible for as long as possible. It is thought by many commentators that the price has been manipulated for many years to be artificially low, and is in no way representative of how much Silver exists in physical form.

For example, on COMEX, the main New York USA exchange for trading silver, there may be more short sales than there is silver to back them up. Again, if this is true, then imagine what would happen if those sellers were all forced to buy silver on the open market to meet their promises? And more importantly, would they even be able to? In the USA, there is even a Silver Users Association, representing the viewpoint of businesses that consume silver, and lobbying government when necessary to protect those interests. They successfully managed to delay, but not stop, the introduction of the first ever Silver investment fund, the Barclays iShares Silver ETF in 2006 (for an explanation of ETFs, see the Exchange-Traded Funds chapter).

There are certainly plenty of interesting stories of intrigue and note out there on this subject, and there are many who think that if there is an asset your government preferred you didn't own, well then, it is probably a major asset you should consider owning.

So, hopefully, faced with all of this knowledge, you are now fired up to at least consider diversifying some of your savings into precious metals, so let's look at the main methods available and the major disadvantages of each.

GOLD AND SILVER COINS

As most of the major nations were part of the Gold Standard which ended after World War 1 (1918) there are a huge variety of Gold Coins available to collectors and Gold investors.

These coins were produced by many different nations and can be in high demand with collectors; hence their value can vary over and above that of the underlying gold metal. The great thing for anyone buying these kind of gold coins, not just numismatists (coin collectors), is the fact of holding a piece of real history, of ever-lasting value in your hand.

In addition, many gold producing countries like South Africa, Australia and Canada still produce new gold and silver coins of standard weights.

Gold coins in particular are rarely made from solid (or 24 carat) Gold. This is because gold is, despite its value and inert properties, a soft metal that can scratch or damage fairly easily. To increase the wear of coins, they were traditionally mixed in an alloy with another metal such as copper. For example. Gold sovereigns are 90% Gold.

The same goes for silver coins as with gold, although as Silver is of much lower value these normally constituted the smaller value coins in circulation. These are even easier to find than Gold Coins and remained in use for a much longer period. For example, if you have any old British Shillings dated prior to 1947 these contain silver instead of Nickel.

The great thing about silver coins is that they can often be bought for less than the silver value weight of the coins. This is often true of the base, low value coins of yesteryear where many millions were originally minted.

Advantages of Gold and Silver Coins
• As standard coins, they are of easily recognizable, documented weight and value.

• They are small, portable forms of wealth easily carried on your person in a time of crisis.

» Physical possession of Gold and Silver coins is the ultimate way of retaining your wealth. Only theft (governmental or otherwise) can take your wealth from you.

• Gold and Old Silver coins in the European Union do not attract VAT.

• Good news for British investors is that expert opinion is that the sale of Gold Sovereigns does not attract Capital Gains Tax (CGT) either. This is not something the Inland Revenue would be keen to advertise, but is due to the fact that Sovereigns have a face value of One Pound and therefore still qualify as currency of the realm. They therefore hold huge advantages for British Investors. The same may be true for buying face value gold coinage in the currency of whatever country you live in, although you need to check these rules for yourself.

Disadvantages of Gold and Silver Coins

• Premiums are often higher than other forms of investment outlined later

• Physical possession could make you a target for theft so remember to find a safe hiding place

• New Silver coins can attract VAT in the European Union, and if so should be avoided

• When you come to sell, it might be hard to find a willing buyer at close to the underlying metal price - your coin dealer will offer a similar percentage under the gold price to what he charged you over the gold price, unless your coins are also desirable to collectors.

In summary, visit a reputable coin dealer to make sure you are getting coins that are worth the money, and that you do not pay too much over the underlying value of the metal in the coin. Tell him you are mainly interested in the metal value and not the numismatic element. In this respect, British Sovereigns and South African Krugerrands often seem to have fairly low percentage premiums above the gold value and are universally recognized coins.

Your own government may sometimes also bring out special "limited edition" coin sales that might even include gold bullion coins. These should normally be avoided because the premiums above the underlying metal prices are usually very high. You can often visit coin dealers directly later to purchase the same, or similar coins at much lower premiums. You can always use the internet to check if they are a good deal against published coin dealer prices.

EBay and other auction sites are not particularly recommended since you have no way of verifying a sellers' claim until after you have handed your money over. The prices attained on the internet right now also seem rather high considering the additional risks of not having seen or examined the items beforehand and possible postal loss.

Conversely, E-Bay might turn out to be a good place to sell your coins if there is ever a crisis in the future and Gold is suddenly in great demand again, because you are able to advertise to a worldwide audience at very low cost.

It is also possible to buy coins from many specialist dealers on the internet, but remember to check out the com-missions you'll be paying, insured postage costs and also whether you'll be liable for customs fees on delivery.

Finally, remember what was said earlier, that the US air force issues all of its pilots with 2 gold sovereigns to use in trade if they are shot down. This surely tells us some-thing about the value of owning gold coins in a time of crisis.

GOLD AND SILVER BARS

These have a lot of the advantages and disadvantages of Coins, such as physically owning the metal. Bars are made in various sizes and can be as convenient to own as the coins but there are some other factors to consider.

Advantages of Gold and Silver Bars
• Bullion bars are usually available for really low premiums above the gold or silver price.
• Bullion bars can be easily identified and valued as they are usually hallmarked
• Gold bars do not attract VAT in the EU.

Disadvantages of Gold and Silver Bars

• Silver bars do attract VAT in the EU. No EU investor should consider investing in silver bars because of this rule.

• A bullion bar cannot be split into smaller units for trading.

The same dealer who can sell you coins can normally also sell bullion bars on the same basis. It is also possible to buy bullion bars from many specialist dealers on the internet, but remember to check out the commissions you'll be paying, insured postage costs and also whether you'll be liable for customs fees on delivery.

JEWELERY

Historically the wearing of jewelery probably comes to a large extent from the need to carry your stored wealth with you, be it in the form of rings, necklaces or what-ever.

Now since jewelery is the precious metal item most advertised as being of a certain number of carats, this seems like a good time to explain what a carat is. It is a measure of Gold purity, between 1 and 24, where 24 is the highest quality purity. So, if an item is 24 carat gold, it is over 99% Gold, about as close to pure gold as it is possible to get. If it is 18-carat, it is 75%, 12-carat means 50%, and 9-carat means 37.5% Gold. Many coins are, like Gold sovereigns for example, 90% gold and therefore 22- carat, and hence the different gold hues associated with the different levels of purity, as the rest is made up of base metals. What this means in reality is that if you, have for example, a 9-carat gold ring, you should weigh it then multiply the weight by 0.375 to obtain the weight of gold it contains.

You can then multiply this by the daily price for Gold given in most newspapers to get the approximate value of the ring if you were to sell it today. You might be shocked at how little some of your favorite items are underlying worth compared to how much you paid for them.

As silver is much less valuable silver items are normally of a much higher purity although pure silver is still of-ten too soft for jewelery and thus jewelery is normally made of silver alloys like Sterling Silver. Sterling Silver is 92.5% silver, with the balance made up of something like copper to increase the resilience.

Most jewelery in Europe and the USA is worth a lot less than the retail prices in the shops. If gold and silver even came into demand again, you could probably imagine customers at retail stores no longer taking sales assistants at face value when they say such and such item is "18-carat" for example, and asking them detailed questions about how much it weighs and what the precious metal content actually is.

Other regions such as the Middle East and India place far more emphasis on the actual precious metals value of jewelery. It is only conjecture but perhaps they have more recent examples of financial crises in their histories, which makes them more aware of the inherent value of such items, and Dubai for example is said by some to be a good place to buy high quality gold jewelery at fairly small premiums above the underlying precious metal value.

Advantages of Jewelery
• Jewelery can certainly be the most aesthetically pleasing precious metal option.
• Personal possession of precious metal
• Can be carried upon your person in times of extreme crisis
» Probably safe from government confiscation under all but the most extreme circumstances

Disadvantages of Jewelery
• Large mark-ups above the metal price for extra manufacture and retail costs
• Unlike coins and bars, they are not easily identifiable storage forms of value. Only an expert can probably identify the quality and value of a given gold ring for example.

Jewelery is therefore not recommended beyond its emotional value to the owner but a gold wedding ring is a handy, if you excuse the pun, final backup resource to own in a time of extreme crisis.

OTHER GOLD AND SILVER ITEMS

Here it is worth mentioning other types of Gold and Silver items that people can accumulate. This could be souvenir gold nuggets, gold teeth or, especially in the case of silver, aesthetically pleasing items such as silver tea sets or cutlery that have been passed down through the generations.

While these may often have a value well in excess of the metal value, the point is that they are worth at least the value of the metal they are manufactured from.

Aside from the lack of portability of large items, all the advantages and disadvantages of jewelery apply, and if you do have any such items in the house, it may be well worth weighing them to find out their base metal value for starters.

It is sometimes possible to buy damaged or worn scrap items at well below the value of the metal at junk sales and the like. These can often be a good, cheap way of gaining some precious metals exposure at a fair price.

STORING YOUR GOLD AND SILVER SAFELY

It may be possible for you to visit your bank and say you wish to purchase gold or silver and they can arrange a deal. But watch the terms of the deal closely.

It may also be possible for your bank to arrange storage of any physical gold you already own in a Safe deposit box.

When it comes to Gold storage there are two forms of ownership to take into account and the difference be-tween these two forms of ownership is vital, as they could mean the difference between something and nothing in the event of a crisis.

Allocated Storage

The gold belongs to you and the bank is only acting as an agent holding it on your behalf. If you really want your bank to manage a gold investment for you, then it needs to be held like this because it's the only way you are protected if the bank collapses.

Unallocated Storage

You only bought a share in the banks' gold. This is not desirable at all since the bank still has the rights over the gold and you are only another creditor of the bank. The bank can freely sell that gold in the event of an emergency to pay its creditors, including you (join the queue!).

Advantages of Bank Storage
• Could be a fair deal, depending on the fees.
• Depending on what the future holds it could be safer than storing them at your home

Disadvantages of Bank Storage
• A bank's primary business nowadays is the issuing of currency not managing gold. They will charge yearly storage fees for holding your gold.
• In 1933, when the USA confiscated all the nations' gold where was the first place they looked?
 That's right, in bank safety deposit boxes. It was even made illegal to open a bank safety deposit box without a warden present.
• If your gold is unallocated, then a bank collapse is a disaster, but even if it's not would you trust an organization in this state to safely guard your gold? Consider further that bank collapses normally accompany the inflationary situations that make gold a desirable asset to own.

The alternative is a storage option of your own choice, be it a hidden safe in your home, or even a hole in the ground. The large number of archaeological gold and silver hoards dating from hundreds or thousands of years ago that are found are probably evidence of the crises our ancestors had to face and the lengths they had to go to guard their wealth.

Fortunately compared to our ancestors, we now have many more options to safeguard our wealth by linking at least some of our investments to gold and silver. These investments can often protect your wealth outside of your local government jurisdiction, which can be another useful factor in their favor. So we will now be looking at paper and electronic forms of gold and silver.

INVESTMENT FUNDS AND MINING STOCKS

If you have a financial advisor advising you on your investments and you mentioned a gold, silver angle he would likeliest mention investing in a Gold or Natural Resources fund, but you need to be aware that this usually really means a fund investing in mining companies. Merrill Lynch Gold Unit Trust for example, has magnificent performance figures over prior years but much of this fund is invested in gold mining companies and not gold itself. This introduces many extra variables into the game, as well as the higher fund management fees that you will be paying.

To minimize these fees you could then decide to invest directly into mining stocks listed on the stock market yourself and as the two investment forms are very similar we will consider them together.

Well in addition to worrying about the price of the underlying commodity you have to ask the same business questions you would ask of any other corporation e.g. is the company well-run? Are the countries in which the mines operate free and open or could the mines be confiscated? Is the mine environmentally conscious or are campaigners trying to get it closed down?

Yes if you pick the right mining companies who dis-cover huge reserves of gold or silver then the price of these stocks will rise dramatically in excess of underlying commodity prices, but the simple fact to remember is that you are investing in stocks. As famous author Mark Twain once allegedly commented, "A mine is a hole in the ground with a liar at the top". It is possible to make huge profits in mining companies but you really need to do your homework.

Another thing to be aware of when investing stocks, especially gold stocks, is something called "production hedging". In practice, this means the selling of future mining production that has not yet being dug out of the mine, at a price acceptable to both parties, based on to-day's gold price.

In a falling gold price market, this could be a spectacularly profitable decision, but in a rising gold price market, a really bad business decision has been made be-cause you are forced to sell your production at yester-days much lower price. The key thing to realize is that this is another business factor that could affect your in-vestment value. The solution? Always look for "unhedged" mining companies.

On the Stock Market, small mining companies in particular also often suffer from wide bid-offer spreads. In case you're not sure what the bid-offer spread is, this is when a share price is listed in the newspaper as being, say, 9p per share, but when you come to buy the price is 9.25p, and when you come to sell you are offered 8.75p. It occurs because the Market Maker is buying and selling these shares, making a profit by quoting a lower price to those wanting to sell their shares to him and a higher price to those wanting to buy from him.

The bid offer spread is one of the least understood parts of investing and hence one of the sneakiest ways for you to lose money without realizing it. Only buy or sell when the bid offer spread is tight - IE there is not much percentage difference between the selling price and buying price because then you know you are getting a fair deal. It is not uncommon to see shares (especially penny mining shares) listed at, say, 1.25p to sell and 2.5p to buy. This is a disaster transaction to be avoided at all* costs - the share needs to double for you to get your money back and that doesn't even include other fees.

If you do fancy investing in mining stocks then there are plenty of experts out there who produce newsletters with investing recommendations and who have proven successful track records along with great knowledge on the mining nuances of terms such as "provable re-sources" and the cost calculations involved in getting ore out of the ground and processed. So, if you are interested then you should do some research yourself to find a newsletter that suits you and ride on the back of one these heavyweights.

The one caveat to this would be to consider investing in a miner such as the world's largest mining company, BHP Billiton. Large mining companies are hugely diversified operations with many streams of income from various commodities (even a gold mining company will produce silver and copper as by-products) and various mines throughout the world, so are not so affected by one bad decision or unforeseen circumstance in any one area. Okay performance is unlikely to be so heart stopping as it would be with a small miner either, but it depends on your own investing aims.

Mining stocks are listed on many stock exchanges throughout the world, especially the USA, Australia, Canada South Africa and more latterly the London AIM (Alternative Investment Market).

Advantages of Gold Mining Stocks

• Direct investing into mining companies gives you geared returns on the gold price increase. For ex ample if a miner makes $20 profit per ounce when gold is priced at $600, all other things being equal he will make $40 profit per ounce if gold rises to $620. What other business can double profits like that?
» Mining companies could discover new reserves that boost company value too
• Investment funds are very diversified and give you more diversified coverage than you could ever attain investing on your own account
• Investing in foreign-listed gold mining stocks can put your wealth outside of local government jurisdiction

Disadvantages of Gold Mining Stocks

« The geared returns can work both ways - a fall in mineral prices can wipe out profitability altogether.
« Mining companies are subject to business or political variances outside of gold and silver prices.
• Direct investment into one or two companies does not give you a very diversified portfolio
• Small mining companies can be very illiquid to trade on world markets

There is one more way of accessing mining stocks and that is through Exchange Traded Funds (ETFs) which are explained in the following chapter.

EXCHANGE-TRADED FUNDS

Exchange-Traded Funds or ETFs are the new kid on the block combining the pooled investment potential of Unit Trusts with much lower fees. They are listed on the stock market and as such are tradable in the same way as ordinary shares.

From a Stocks and Shares point of view ETFs are exciting because they have the potential to offer a much broader range of investments. Already you can invest in various hitherto unavailable indexes directly such as Chinese or Korean stock indexes but the great thing is that there are now even opportunities to invest in commodities such as gold and silver. This has the potential to diversify or switch your portfolio more broadly than you could ever have done so in the past.

If you have a financial advisor, then depending on the type of financial advisor you use they may not recommend or know about ETFs simply because they do not pay enough, if any commission. This fact alone should tell you what a comparatively good deal ETFs are.

There are two ETF types of interest to Gold and Silver investments, and in both cases you can buy shares in the ETF itself through the stock market and join the party.

Some of these ETFs are simply tracking the gold or silver price. There are several Gold ETFs and at least one Silver ETF of this type you can invest in. You can check out ETF Securities, Barclay's iShares or Lyxor Gold, to name a few. Yearly fees are normally low. The funds either invest in the metals and store it in a vault or invest on the metals futures markets. Popular preference is for those funds that store the metal in a vault because your in-vestment is more closely matched to the actual metal.

Other ETFs are simply buying a basket all of the mining stocks listed on a given stock market. These have the dual advantage of allowing investing in mining companies and achieving greater diversification than investing alone could ever do. Some of the ETFs you could consider include AMEX Gold Bugs and iShares CDN Gold, both listed in the USA.

At this point, you should consider the importance of looking for the cheapest online broker when investing, and in this respect, for those in the UK or EU, the UK-based broker Selftrade is worthy of consideration - their commission per deal is £12.50, which is not in itself the cheapest but they do have a price improvement promise which often seems to undercut the official bid, offer spread. Their accounts are available to non-UK residents who pass their ID requirements, and at time of writing this you can email

And if you live in the UK and want to invest through your tax-free ISA (Individual Savings Account) or SIPP (Self-invested Pension Plan), then Selftrade is also currently offering to rebate transfer fees up to £100 if you transfer your plan(s) to them and the same deal above about emailing It is guaranteed that your email address will remain confidential and not be passed on to any other parties or used for marketing purposes.

Advantages of ETFs
« The costs are also much lower then comparable
 Unit trusts. For example, Merrill Gold Unit Trust has at time of writing, an initial charge of 5% and an annual charge of 1.75%. A near-equivalent ETF has an annual charge of 0.5% and the normal costs associated with purchase of a stock on the stock market. a For UK investors, ETFs unlike shares do not attract stamp duty
• Gold and Silver ETFs are passive tracker investments in the main so performance will almost match the equivalent index
• You do not have any personal storage costs to pay and the pooled storage cost among all investors will be a lot cheaper
• For European Union investors. Silver ETFs are a way of legally owning Silver bullion without paying VAT

Disadvantages of ETFs
• Smaller ETFs are very illiquid and it can sometimes be difficult to get an on-line quote
• ETFs tend to be passive tracker investments in the main so performance will almost match the equivalent index - yes, this was also down as an advantage and in the main it probably is, but some may think you can do better by direct investing in mining stocks or spread betting.
• The Metals are not physically in your possession should you need the money quickly.

Overall ETFs definitely have a place in a diversified Metals portfolio, especially for UK investors, who can invest using their tax-free ISA allowance. This is covered more in the book Successful Tax-Free ISA Investing by the same author.

SPREAD BETTING

Here you are opening an account with a gambling website and wagering on whether the price of your chosen commodity will rise or fall in a given timescale. Bets are normally places at a price per unit, and that price per unit is multiplied by the units you win by or lose by to calculate your profit or loss on the wager.

Advantages of Spread Betting
• In many countries, gambling is classified as a leisure activity and thus profits or losses are not taxable transactions. This could be a great benefit.
• There are none of the physical costs associated with ownership of the metal.
• Spread Betting could allow you to play short term movements in the metals pricing markets to your advantage. For example you could buy and sell on the same day with low transaction costs.

Disadvantages of Spread Betting

• Your Investment is quite far removed from owning physical gold. In the event of a severe crisis where you need money on hand right now, this could be a problem.
• You need to learn about and understand the vagaries and rules of spread betting, aside from any knowledge you may have about gold or silver.
• Your bets are normally placed at a unit per point loss or profit. E.g. £5 for every cent gold falls or rises. If a bet goes against you big time, you may lose a lot more than you originally invested.

If you are still interested then you could check out 1C Index or Cantor, among the many companies out there offering this service, but before you begin investing serious money in spreadbetting, you could find out whether it suits your style by taking advantage of one of the offers available where you test the systems by either trading for free using imaginary funds, or trading at only, say, 1 pence per point.

THE FUTURES MARKET

Gold and silver are traded on the futures markets like any other commodity with forward delivery dates and pricing based on what the majority investors expect gold to be at that time.

In case you're not sure what futures are, this is the market where a farmer or miner agrees to sell his forthcoming production at a certain price, to be delivered on a certain date. This contract can then be sold and resold by any number of investors. Whoever is holding the contract on the final delivery date is expected to take possession of the commodity in question. As an investor, you wouldn't be interested in the delivery, just in trading the contract on for profit prior to the delivery date.

Advantages of the Futures Market
• Could allow you to play short term movements in the metals pricing markets to your advantage.
• There are none of the physical costs associated with ownership of the metal.
• A lot of futures brokers allow you to invest "on margin", which means that you can put down, say, £500 and invest up to £10,000. If a bet goes your way big time, you can make an awful lot of money.

Disadvantages of the Futures Market

• Your Investment is removed from owning physical gold. In the event of a severe crisis where you need money on hand right now, or the futures market closes for some reason, this could be a problem.
• You need to learn about and understand the vagaries and rules of how the futures markets work, aside from any knowledge you may have about gold or silver.
• A lot of futures brokers allow you to invest "on margin", which means that you can put down, say, £500 and invest up to £10,000. If a bet goes against you big time, you may lose a lot more than you originally invested.

There are many companies out there offering this service. Interactive Brokers is one internet-based one that offers full online trading facilities at a reasonable price.

DERIVATIVES

Here's where you can move into really esoteric investments.

If you know a bit about the stock market then you may have heard of things like Options or Contracts for Difference (CFDs). It is possible to play the same moves on Gold and Silver mining stocks or commodity prices in the same way as it is possible to do on other asset classes.

These are called derivatives, because they are investment markets derived from the underlying asset prices, be it stock or commodity prices.

Advantages of Derivatives
• Could allow you to play short term movements in the metals pricing markets to your advantage.
• There are none of the physical costs associated with ownership of the metal.
• Options and derivatives are a geared play on an asset class movement. A small price move in your favour can multiply the value of your original investment many times over.

Disadvantages of Derivatives

• Your Investment is removed from owning physical gold. In the event of a severe crisis where you need money on hand right now, or the market closes for some reason, this could be a problem.
• You need to learn about and understand the vagaries and rules of how the markets work, aside from any knowledge you may have about gold or silver.
• Options and derivatives are normally a geared play on an asset class movement. Even a small move against you can destroy your original investment and leave you owing a lot more besides.

To summarize, derivatives may not be the best investing move for the introductory gold and silver investors this book is intended for. They require a lot of specialist knowledge and if you really want to find out more about options trading, and other related investment classes, then it is recommended that you read specialist literature and become comfortable with the concepts before risking any of your investment capital.

PERTH MINT CERTIFICATES

Perth Mint certificates are a new way of buying title to Australian Gold through certificates. The Perth Mint has existed since 1899 and is backed by the State government of Western Australia.

They offer both Allocated and Unallocated storage. These two options were described in the section on Gold Storage and you may remember that Allocated is the recommended option. Allocated attracts a fabrication and storage fee in this case, but unallocated does not.

These can only be bought through official brokers of Perth Mint certificates. Research as of 2006 shows that they do not all charge the same fees so it is recommended you visit the list of recommended brokers on their website and investigate thoroughly. For example, Pacific Capital quoted a lesser price than Gold and Silver Investments, even though the latter was a more local dealer for the author (UK and Ireland). You should be able to use any dealer you wish.

There are a lot of ID requirements for people wishing to invest in Perth Mint Certificates, including a potential need for notarised documents from a lawyer, so this might be something else you need to consider in your investing plans.

Advantages of Perth Mint Certificates
- Western Government-backed guarantee
- For the likes of US or European investors for example your Investinent lies far away from local   government jurisdiction
- Low Fees
- Offers allocated storage
- No VAT on Silver purchases for EU buyers

Disadvantages of Perth Mint Certificates
• High initial investment required (10,000 US$)
• Can only cash in the bonds in large units
• Only a limited number of brokers retail this service
• The service is paper-based and not internet based so it may take a while to get your money back when you decide to cash in, and, unless you live in Perth your metals could be very hard to access in a time of crisis.

Conclusion is that those looking to squirrel away a large sum for long-term investment purposes may find these the best investing option. Their Australian location may also appeal to those subject to other government jurisdictions. The Perth Mint does in fact advertise that no taxes are payable on purchases or sales of precious metals in Australia, and that Australia allows free movement of precious metals in and out of Australia.

Perth Mint also have a Gold-tracking product similar to an ETF listed on the Australian Stock Exchange (code ZAUWBA), but in this case it is traded as a warrant. In case you are not aware, a Warrant is a type of derivative, and is actually the right to buy a product (usually shares in a company), within a given-time period, at a certain price. In this case,-however, each warrant gives the right to buy 1 ounce of fine gold from Gold Corporation, the owners of the .Perth Mint, and can be exercised by the holder at any time up 31st December 2013. .

ELECTRONIC GOLD AND SILVER

Electronic gold and more lately electronic silver, is a superb idea that could only ever have been made possible by the internet. The theory is that you exchange your money with an internet-based organization that then gives you an account containing an equivalent number of gold units.

These gold units are your bank account and theoretically backed by an equivalent amount of gold held on storage somewhere.

The gold units you hold can be held or exchanged for services bought over the internet. If you hold the units, you will have to pay a storage fee for your gold, although as with ETFs this will be less than trying to go it alone. Normally, storage will also be allocated, and you might remember that this is the preferred storage option, since it means there is some real metal out there that be-longs you.

You are normally free to exchange your gold back into a variety of national currencies at any time, at the prevailing gold exchange rate less a small fee, either fixed or a percentage. Some providers allow you to retain your national currency with them; others will pay it back to you. The ease with which you are able to withdraw your currency and receive it back in your bank account is also something else you may need to consider.

The Major Fees to Consider are:

Storage Cost
Usually quoted monthly as a percentage, or a fixed amount. The fixed amount is normally the best deal for larger holdings.

Buy Transaction Cost
Same as with coins, there will be a bid-offer spread, where you pay, say, 2% over spot price to buy. Also remember to investigate whether there will be any other fees applicable to your situation, for example, personal bank fees if you live in Norway and the digital currency provider only accepts dollars.

Sell Transaction Cost
Just the same as with coins, there will be a bid-offer spread where you receive, say, 2% under spot price when you sell. Also remember to investigate whether there will be any other fees applicable to your situation, for example, money transfer fees if you need your money in Norwegian Krone and the e-gold provider only pays out dollars.

Possibilities for use as digital currency
Would you like to spend your gold directly on other products instead of exchanging into national currency? If so then this could be useful, as more and more internet retailers are offering this as an

option. Remember to investigate whether the fees are suited to the type of transactions you think you'll be making.

Advantages of Electronic Gold and Silver
• Internet-based, so a very accessible product with low costs
• Pooled investment, so secure storage costs are less than going it alone
• Your investment can be stored safely outside of local government jurisdiction
• Easy to buy and sell just by logging in to your PC
• Can be used as a medium of exchange in business transactions, and can even work out cheaper than bank conversion of national currencies

Disadvantages of Electronic Gold and Silver
• You are trusting a third party organization with your wealth, so you need to be sure that they are definitely holding the relevant amount of gold to meet all their depositors. If a particular organization ever gets into trouble, your gold and entire wealth could be at risk.
• Governments may target digital currency providers because they feel they are missing out on tax revenue or that their National currencies are being undermined. Ironically, the USA, long-regarded as the "land of the free", is currently leading the way in this respect. How this affects your savings is uncertain.
• Unlike credit card payments, payments with digital currency are usually irreversible. Most providers do make this major difference clear up front, so if there are any issues concerning a transaction e.g. faulty or non-delivered goods, then it would be up to you to chase up the situation with whatever legal backing is necessary. EBay has banned the use of E-Gold and allegedly cancels any auction offering E-Gold as a payment method, although some critics claim that this is mainly done to protect their vested interest in Paypal, their own online payments system.

Before going any further, some readers may ask why the fact that electronic currency providers, unlike banks and bank deposits, aren't regulated or financially backed by the government in any way has not been listed as a major disadvantage. Well, to be honest, part of the attraction of gold is the independence of national borders and constraints that holding it should bring. Considering past histories of government mismanagement of national currencies and confiscation of wealth, who can you really truly trust to look after your hard-earned money?

The major people involved with the well-known digital currency businesses are all greatly enthusiastic about the subject of gold, 100% believe in gold as the one true store of value and often write articles displaying their depth of knowledge on the subject. So when it comes to trust, could you really consider them to be any less trustworthy than the average politician?

There are a lot of providers out there, but as a British citizen living in the European Union a lot of them were found to be heavily slanted towards the US market. For example, only accepting payment in dollars or paying out in dollars. One name that springs to mind as being of sound principle but US-based is "Liberty Dollar", as the name implies. Another is the Gold Dinar system based in the Middle East.

One more thing you will have to consider is the application criteria for your chosen provider. In order to meet with government money laundering regulations and the like, many providers require multiple copies of documents for proof of you and your address, and perhaps even notarized documents from your bank or lawyer. This can add extra administration, cost and time to opening an account.

We'll now cover some of the main providers that cater for citizens throughout the world and do not discriminate against non-US citizens, by which it is meant non-US citizens who otherwise might end up paying extra bank transfer fees, etc.

E-GOLD

E-Gold was one of the first organizations to offer this service. It was started up by a Dr. Jackson who strongly believes in the gold story, and that gold is due a come-back as the trusted medium of exchange. E-gold started out in the USA and have since moved their jurisdiction to Nevis in the West Indies.

They offer deposit facilities and also heavily promote the use of e-gold for payments. There could be an exciting future for e-gold, but unfortunately, they are having to deal with various allegations made by the US Government, including aiding and abetting illegal activity and running an unregistered banking institution.

Some critics wonder whether the reason they are being chased is the alleged use of e-Gold for fraudulent purposes, or whether it is an attempt to stop US citizens from dumping the ailing dollar, placing their wealth out-side of US jurisdiction and using a truly international hard currency.

The next important point is that e-Gold continues to operate as a legitimate business and is not being singled out by the US Government, as right now they seem to be chasing a lot of internet gold and silver providers including the aforementioned Liberty Dollar scheme. Any US citizen should probably be monitoring the actions of their government very carefully right now, as they seem to curtailing a lot of the principles attached to free movement of wealth, internet gambling being another example. As fair or unfair as this ongoing saga may be, if you are a US citizen you might want to consider your own intended usage of any digital currency provider because of government actions. Nobody can possibly predict future legislation and its effect on business dealings, least of all this book.

People conducting business on the internet may find an e-gold account especially useful because of its slant to-wards being used as a medium of exchange, and even traditional businesses in countries with high inflation could use it in future to agree prices with customers in terms of gold regardless of what happens to their national currency.

E-Gold have had such success with Gold, that they are now offering e-Silver, e-Platinum and e-Palladium too.

The process for transferring money into and out of E-Gold involves the use of separate payment providers. Authorized and recommended organizations are listed on their website. There is a fee of approximately 2% for transfer of funds in and transfer of funds out, plus you may also be liable to local bank fees. Different payment providers seem to have different fees, so it is well worth finding the best one for you. This system is quite flexible in that you can use a variety of payment systems to transfer money in or out, such as a credit card or Paypal account.

E-Gold also charge a storage fee for the days in which you own precious metals within their system. This is currently 1% per annum. This system of charging could work well for smaller amounts, or where your metal is used as a medium for exchange and thus many days your account holding is zero.

GOLDMONEY

This is the brainchild of highly-respected gold watcher James Turk. You pay a fee only when you buy, although this does seem to mean that the buy bid price is higher than some other alternatives.

Goldmoney has been structured with a cast iron guarantee that there will always be 100% gold backing of every unit of currency (called "goldgrams" in this case) in circulation, and they claim that some others such as E-gold and Perth Mint do not have the same cast-iron guarantees in their small print. Whether this is true or not is hard to say, as for an ordinary investor the small-print is difficult to understand, but the discussions and articles available make interesting reading when deciding on the safety of providers you are considering.

Goldmoney, like e-gold, also tries to offer the use of Goldmoney as a medium of payment. This however is not very heavily used right now, and the majority of investors are gold bugs simply buying gold and silver and holding it.

Monthly storage fees are also low. At time of writing, for gold, it is a flat 1,10 of a gram of gold per month, or about $2.43 per month. This is regardless of holding size, so is an extremely good deal for larger holdings that are not traded regularly.

If you are a US citizen, then you could find their regular savings "Gold Accumulation Plan" to be a winner. It works on the basis of the time-tested investing concept of unit cost averaging, where a fixed monthly amount saved buys x number of goldgrams at the spot rate + 1.9%. As the author is a British citizen, it is aggrieving that they don't yet offer this superb plan in other countries, as this is one of the best deals for investing in gold found anywhere. Enquiries indicate that this service may be in operation at some point in the future.

What could appeal to British or EU citizens about Gold-money is that it is Jersey-based. You may trust and understand the rules of Jersey more than those of the Caribbean or Panama. This is not to say that other organizations are unsafe. A US-citizen may just as easily understand Panama and believe it to be much safer than Jersey.

GoldMoney recently introduced a Silver option, and this represents an excellent opportunity for European Union buyers to buy Silver bullion without legally paying any VAT. More latterly they also introduced the ability to hold the national currencies of Dollars, Pounds or Euros in your Goldmoney account and receive interest on it. You can then switch your holding between any of the five denominations (including the two metals), as you see fit.

Knowing that it's the fees that make investors poor and brokers rich, you are probably best off not utilizing this feature. The fees will quickly eat into your returns, and a buy-and-hold strategy is probably best.

Payment into GoldMoney is by bank transfer. Payment out can be made by direct bank transfer and often these can be free of charge for example if you live in the UK and receive your currency in Pounds to a British bank account using the UK BACs system. If your preferred currency is not Pounds Dollars Canadian Dollars or Euros GoldMoney also offers the use of Payment Providers to help transfers into and from your chosen currency although there may be other fees on top to consider.

One other aspect of GoldMoney worthy of mention is that if you account is not logged into for 12 years the ownership of your gold reverts to Goldmoney. Okay, it sounds unlikely but consider what would happen if you died and never told anybody about your holding or even if you were unable to use the internet for 12 years due to some kind of accident or national crisis.

Overall a highly respected organization with the reputation of a known "gold-watcher" behind it. Even if you don't buy Goldmoney then Turk's articles are available for free on the website and make interesting reading.

Electronic Gold and Silver

BULLIONVAULT

Founded by Paul Tustain, BullionVault sits somewhere between Goldmoney, for safety and Gold storage and the trading services mentioned earlier. Bullionvault is UK-based, although an additionally interesting feature is the ability to store your gold in their New York, London or Zurich gold vaults. Dependent on which country you are a citizen of, you will probably feel most comfortable placing your gold outside of that country so that is not subject to your local government jurisdiction, so top marks for considering that feature.

An interesting aspect of the three separate vaults is that these could be considered as separate currencies in their own right. For example, if at some point in the future there was a repeat of the 1930s US Gold confiscation, gold stored in a New York Vault might become priced significantly lower than gold stored in a Zurich vault, as US holders try to sell and place their gold outside their own jurisdiction.

BullionVault allows you to buy and sell Gold on their impressive looking trading platform, where buyers and sellers of gold from each vault can meet and state their required selling buying prices, so if you are more inclined to hold gold, occasionally sell on a dip, then buy in again later, then this could well be the best service for you.

Their fees for transactions and monthly storage are really low too, so they are very worthy of investigation. The storage fee is currently $4 per month fixed, regardless of holding size, and only payable for the months in which you held Gold.

Again, Bullionvault has proved popular with Gold Bugs accumulating gold for the future financial crisis they believe is in the offing. Payment in to BullionVault is by bank transfer.

Payment out is by bank wire transfer to your chosen bank account. A fee of approximately $30 is charged for this transfer, although there may be possibilities for UK residents to request a BACs transfer instead, which can take a few days but will not attract a fee.

There is no Silver option. This may be something to do with Bullion Vault being UK-based and the UK charging VAT on silver sales, which could, to many observers, seem to be another example of government getting in the way of free trade.

BullionVault are currently offering a free gram of gold to all new account openings, which you can then use to experiment with trading in their system. Even if you open an account, you are not committed in any way, so well worth trying out to see if it's for you

OTHER WAYS TO INVEST

Okay, so new we've covered the major ways of investing in Gold and Silver, but can you think of any other ways that could pay off in the future?

One suggestion would be to consider buying Internet domain names with a precious metals angle. These could either be developed into relevant websites on the subject that generate cash using Google Advertisements and/or Affiliate Links, or just parked with a domain parking service in the hope of resale at a profit. If you're not quite sure what I mean, check out. the two sites connected to this book:

It is fair to assume that if there is ever a financial crisis and Gold and Silver once again come to the fore, then relevant domain names, especially those with traffic, could be worth a lot more, or be more cash generative than their yearly domain registration and web hosting fees are costing.

Should you wish to experiment with this route, then at the two websites listed above you will find some of the cheapest domain name registers that you can find and buy your domain names from.

There are probably many other ideas out there that have not even been thought of yet, but could prove to be spectacularly profitable. It just needs your own creativity!

GOLD AND SILVER INVESTING SCAMS

It would be unwise to complete this book without warning you about some of the major scams being perpetrated today. The sad thing is that many of these scams use the worldwide reputation of value and wealth that precious metals, especially Gold, represent as a way to lure naive investors into parting with their cash.

Firstly, never buy gold of uncertain value from unknown sources. This could include jewelery from street traders or even coins from internet auction sellers with no prior sales record. There is simply too much at risk to do otherwise, unless you really feel that the lower price you are paying justifies the risk. In most, if not all cases, it will not, so when buying physical gold, always buy from reputable, well-established sources with good feedback.

Secondly, if a deal looks too good to be true, it probably is. The price of gold in a variety of currencies is listed everywhere daily, so anyone with gold knows its approximate value, therefore why would they offer to sell it to you cheaply? Often people believe they have bought gold bars, later to find that they are lead inside, as lead is a similar weight. Again, to be safe here, only consider buying only from reputable sources where you can go for redress if anything goes wrong.

The internet, abounding with opportunities, while also fraught with dangers is the new wild west of the 21st century, and has also brought forth new avenues for criminals. One of the most common of these is a Gold Investing scam. These scammers play on the fact that people have heard about digital precious metal-backed currencies, but do not have much knowledge about how they really work. Many of these scammers can be found advertising on the right-hand side of the Google search engine in the Google Ads section if you make a Gold-related search, making outlandish claims such as "make V-i to 5% per day" or "double your money in 30 days".

If you are happy that your PC is protected against things like viruses and other worm software infecting it, then you could try visiting some of these sites to familiarize yourself with the type of cons being perpetrated. Furthermore, every click from Google costs these scammers money, and that can be no bad thing either. Google are blameless here, as their Adwords is an excellent service for legitimate businesses and individuals to reach their target audience and there is no way they could be considered accountable for the actions of a criminal minority.

After clicking on the ad, what you'll often then find is a credible-looking website, with heavy use of financial terms and acronyms such as HYIP (High Yield Investment Program), that don't really mean much, along with outlandish claims about how you will get rich by starting with a small sum, like, say $50. This is often backed up by some unintelligible diagram showing gold being routed between various parties and somehow ending up in your account. Even after reading it carefully, you usually still don't understand how the money is made, and searching around the site for real contact details such as a name, address or telephone number throw up very little, if anything relevant.

Please don't ever be conned by these websites or even dubious emails, often from places like Nigeria, offering you the chance to make instant, huge sums of money through gold, silver, digital currency or whatever. If it looks too good to be true, and you can't understand how it works, then it is most probably best to avoid it.

Truth is, if anyone can truly find an investment that returns even 1, 2% per day, the best approach would be to keep quiet until you owned all the gold in the entire world, which, with compounding actually probably wouldn't take as long as you think!

The other sad thing is that E-gold is often the route for this illegally-earned money because it's harder to trace and will cost too much money for the victims to take the perpetrators to court, assuming you ever even find out who the perpetrators are.

E-gold are blameless, as they do make clear up front the irreversible nature of their payments system, but it may affect their credibility longer term, as many potential future users are put off by their lack of knowledge and bad first experience of the world of digital currency.

There are plenty of sites out there full of sad cases of people sharing with others their experiences of how their money has gone, with no replies and no money back. Given the fact th.a.t very few of us, if any ever pet the right financial l-raining in our early years including schooling, to prepare us for the serious financial decisions we'll, have to make in. our adult lives is it a wonder so many naive and trusting .people can be conned by such schemes?

The overriding advice here is to only invest with reputable and well-established Gold sites.

Internet Auction Site Scams

While Internet auction sites are a highly recommended resource for buying many many things, precious metals, especially Gold, are probably not among them.

When you are trading something like Gold, it is important to know you are buying from a reputable source, with comeback if anything is wrong with your purchase. Aside from this, you also have to consider postal costs and other costs.

If you ever do find yourself buying something from the likes on E-Bay then follow a few simple guidelines. Make sure you pay using Paypal, and that your account is funded using a credit card. This gives you the most protection to get your money back if anything goes wrong with the transaction such as the goods not turning up or being not as described.

Another scam to be aware of is when selling items of your own on E-Bay. E-Bay are mentioned here specifically, not because E-Bay is in any way a fraudulent site, but mainly because of its major associations with its payment processing company Paypal and the, lack of understanding of how It works by sellers. Often buyers from. strange countries far from your own will bid on your items and pay using Paypal. After a few weeks, they will register non-arrival of your item even though. you know you sent it and it most probably arrived fine.

Under such circumstances they will claim, for and eventually receive a refund from Paypal, and Paypal will then take the money back from you. Unless you took out adequate insurance on the item, which the buyer should pay for, and successfully claim for your loss from the Post Office then you. are the loser. You are warned about this so you can make a clear decision about offering Paypal as a payment option when selling valuable items such as Gold coins.

SUMMARY

Traditionally, holding gold meant either Gold Coins or jewelery, stored either in your home or local bank, but the internet and electronic trading platforms on it have opened up a new world of Gold and Silver investing to the normal man on the street.

Many previously closed ways of investing in gold easily, such as share-dealing or futures trading are now available, but it has also spawned spread betting and the completely new concept of digital currency.

In the case of digital currency, the declining value of national currencies and rising worldwide internet access could see this new medium for storing wealth and facilitating trade come to the fore and we may yet only be in the early days of a new monetary paradigm.

Armed with the knowledge that these options are avail-able, you should feel confident about investing in gold and silver in the ways that best suit your needs and at the lowest fees.

And now it's time to reiterate that this publication is not directly inducing you to invest or not invest in any particular product, merely to identify opportunities to invest more cheaply, so that more of your money remains your own and secondly to identify possible areas of precious metals investment that are unknown to the majority of investors yet offer great scope to diversify your portfolio and improve your returns.

U. S. Mint Information: (Courtesy of the United States Mint)

American Eagle Gold Bullion Coins

Authorized by the Bullion Coin Act of 1985, American Eagle Gold Bullion Coins quickly became one of the world's leading gold bullion investment coins. Produced from gold mined in the United States, American Eagles are imprinted with their gold content and legal tender "face" value. An American Eagle's value is based on the market price of its metal content, plus a small premium to cover coinage and distribution.

American Eagles use the durable 22 karat standard established for gold circulating coinage over 350 years ago. They contain their stated amount of pure gold, plus small amounts of alloy. This creates harder coins that resist scratching and marring, which can diminish resale value.

Minted to exacting standards, the obverse (front) design is inspired by what's often considered one of America's most beautiful coins: Augustus Saint-Gaudens' celebrated $20 gold piece, minted from 1907-1933. The reverse design, by sculptor Miley Busiek, features a male eagle carrying an olive branch flying above a nest containing a female eagle and her hatchlings.

Government Guarantee

What truly sets American Eagles apart is that they are the only bullion coins whose weight, content and purity are guaranteed by the United States Government. Investors can buy them with confidence, knowing the coins contain their stated amount of gold. In addition, long-term savers can include American Eagles in their Individual Retirement Accounts (IRAs).

Investing in Gold

Ever since its discovery 5,000 years ago, gold has been treasured for its unmatched luster, beauty and intrinsic value. Today, gold continues to enjoy widespread appeal as an investment and storehouse of value. Gold is an internationally recognized monetary and financial asset held in reserve by major governments. It is so rare that all the gold ever mined could fit into a cube measuring just 20 yards on each side. Most importantly, gold can play a role in diversifying an investment portfolio, since it can move independently of stocks and bonds. What's more, gold is a tangible asset - one whose beauty and artistry you can literally hold in your hands. When purchased in the form of legal tender bullion coins, gold can be affordable, as well as easy to buy and store. Americans purchase more American Eagle Gold Bullion Coins than any other gold coin. Produced by the United States Mint, Department of the Treasury, these coins are available in four denominations.

Easy to Buy and Sell

An important measure of any investment is its liquidity: How easy is it to resell? United States Government backing means that like the dollar, American Eagle Bullion Coins are accepted in major investment markets worldwide. They are also the most widely traded bullion coins in America, affording investors narrow spreads between buy and sell prices.

It's easy to track the value of American Eagle Bullion Coins. Most major newspapers report the daily price of gold. An American Eagle's value is based on the market price of its metal content, plus a small premium to cover coinage and distribution costs.

You can purchase American Eagle Gold Bullion Coins from most major coin and precious metals dealers, as well as brokerage houses and participating banks. Click here for a list of authorized dealers. They are minted in four weights - 1/10, 1/4, 1/2 and 1 ounce - to fit a variety of budgets. The smaller sizes also make affordable and thoughtful gifts.

A collectible proof version of the American Eagle Gold Bullion Coin is available directly from the United States Mint.

American Eagle Silver Bullion Coins are affordable investments, beautiful collectibles, thoughtful gifts and memorable incentives or rewards. Above all, as legal tender, they're the only silver bullion coins whose weight and purity are guaranteed by the United States Government. They're also the only silver coins allowed in an IRA.

Silver has historically been the most affordable precious metal. Since 1986, the United States has minted one-dollar silver coins called "Silver Eagles." Each contains a minimum of one troy ounce of 99.9% pure silver.

The design is based on Adolph A. Weinman's 1916 "Walking Liberty" half dollar, widely considered one of the most beautiful American coins ever minted. Silver Eagles are easy to buy and sell at most coin, precious metal and brokerage companies. Click here for a list of authorized dealers. Prices are based on the market price of silver, plus a small premium to cover minting and distribution costs.

They're the qualities that have made American Eagle Silver Bullion Coins the world's best-selling silver coins.

Tips From The American Numismatic Association:

How to Buy and Sell Gold & Silver

Gold and silver prices have been at or near record levels recently, heightening interest in buying and selling gold and silver coins. Consumers, however, should resist the temptation to make impulse buys or to sell an item before researching its potential value.

The ANA urges everyone to be wary of cold-call solicitations or mobile offices, set up in temporary locations such as motels, offering instant cash for gold and silver coins. Be patient, be informed and don't let anyone pressure you into making impulsive decisions.

Following is a checklist we encourage you to follow before buying or selling gold or silver bullion coins.

The reputation and expertise of your bullion dealer is important.

Your dealer needs to be a respected name in the industry with experience buying and selling bullion in fluctuating markets. ANA dealers must adhere to a strict code of ethics. To locate an ANA bullion dealer, use our Dealer Directory.

Know the actual cost per ounce of precious metals.

Gold, silver, and platinum prices fluctuate daily, so check that day's spot price prior to making a transaction. Expect to pay a higher percentage over melt value for fractional gold pieces (1/10th, 1/4th, and 1/2 ounce) than for one-ounce pieces. Also, American Eagle and Canadian Maple Leaf bullion coins typically have a higher retail price than South African Kruggerrand bullion coins.

Understand the fees and/or commissions involved.

According to the Professional Numismatists Guild, the average retail commission for one-ounce American Eagle or Maple Leaf gold coins is about five or six percent.

Arrange for timely delivery

If immediate delivery is not possible, obtain from the seller in writing specific confirmation about the delivery date. Only then should you execute your order.

Know that all investments come with risks.

If you intend to buy bullion coins for investment purposes, your best protection is to spend time learning about the coins before you buy them. Uninformed buyers who make hasty purchases often overpay. Like any investment, there are no guarantees – and no one can predict with certainty that gold and silver prices will remain at the current levels or continue to appreciate.

Protect against identity theft.

Do not give out credit card numbers or bank account numbers or other private information such as Social Security numbers over the phone to anyone not known to you.

RESOURCE ARTICLES

Glossary of terms

Bullion Coin
A bullion coin is a coin that is valued by its weight in a specific precious metal.

Collector or Rare Coin

The value of a collector or rare coin is based upon the coin's rarity, demand, condition and mintage. A collector or rare coin may be worth more than its bullion value.

Spot price

The spot price is the market price for immediate delivery of a commodity, such as gold, silver or platinum. Melt value: Melt value refers to the basic intrinsic bullion value of a coin if melted and sold.

Spread

The spread is the difference between what a dealer will charge to sell an item and what he will pay to purchase it.

Troy ounce

The troy ounce is the measurement used in the pricing of precious metals such as gold and silver. The troy ounce is 480 grains or exactly 31.1034768 grams.

Ask

The price a seller is willing to accept for a security, also known as the offer price. Along with the price, the ask quote will generally also stipulate the amount of the security willing to be sold at that price.

Bid

An offer made by an investor, a trader or a dealer to buy a security. The bid will stipulate both the price at which the buyer is willing to purchase the security and the quantity to be purchased.

Helpful Reference Materials

The Red Book
Yeoman, R. S., Bresset, Kenneth, ed. Guide Book of United States Coins, Atlanta, GA: Whitman Publishing, LLC, 2008.

The Coin Collector's Survival Manual
5th Edition, Scott A. Travers, New York: Random House, 2006.

Standard Catalog of World Coins, 1901-2000
35th Edition, Iola, Wis.: Krause Publications, Inc., 2007.

Standard Catalog of World Coins, 2001-Date
2nd Edition, Iola, Wis.: Krause Publications, Inc., 2007.

Other Resources

NGC with Current Metal Prices

ANA Consumer Awareness

ANA Dealers - Bullion Specialty
Contact Us - coininfo@money.org buying gold, buying bullion, buying silver, buying coins, investing, investments

This article appeared in November 2009 Consumer Reports Magazine:

Cashing in gold? Here's the catch.

With the price of gold near $1,000 an ounce, ads offering quick cash for gold can be tempting. You usually drop unwanted gold jewelry in a postage-paid envelope and a few days later a check is supposed to arrive in the mail. If you think the amount is too small, send the check back and your jewelry is returned at no charge. Often, we found, the amount may indeed be lower than you'd expect.

Our mystery shoppers sent identical 18-karat chains and pendants (retail price $175; meltdown value about $70) to three gold buyers between mid-May and early July. They also took the gold to jewelry stores and pawn shops in Louisiana, New York, and Texas. The cash-for-gold companies paid 11 to 29 percent of the day's market price for gold; the other venues, about 35 to 70 percent. All the checks arrived a few days after the companies received the jewelry.

What you can do:

Before you sell, make sure jewelry isn't antique and therefore worth more intact than melted down. Then:

Calculate its worth. Note any stamped karat mark, then weigh the piece on a good kitchen scale. Go to the calculator at www.dendritics.com/scales/metal-calc.asp and enter karats and weight to learn the value based on the latest gold price. (Gold is traditionally weighed in penny-weights or troy ounces; the calculator translates.) You can also check gold's price at www.kitco.com.

Call several jewelry stores, coin stores, and pawn shops to ask what they pay for gold. If they won't say, don't do business with them. Because the price of gold fluctuates, call all the stores on the same day. Most gold buyers, including those our shoppers used, offer more for larger amounts of gold and might negotiate. Try for at least 50 percent of meltdown value.

Consider gold parties (guests gather with jewelry; a gold-company rep pays on the spot), refiners (look online for smelters), or online gold buyers (check their standing with the Better Business Bureau).

Investing in Gold? What's the Rush?

Read more in this Series:

- *Investing in Bullion and Bullion Coins*
- *Investing in Collectible Coins*

You see the ads on TV and online, and you hear them on the radio: they tout gold as a solid investment. It's true that people sometimes use gold to diversify their investment portfolio: it can help hedge against inflation and economic uncertainty. But how much gold to buy, in what form, at what price, and from whom, are important questions to answer before you make that investment.

The Federal Trade Commission (FTC), the nation's consumer protection agency, says if you are interested in buying gold, do some digging before investing. Some gold promoters don't deliver what they promise, and may push people into an investment that isn't right for them.

All Gold is Not Created Equal

You can buy gold in a variety of forms:

Gold Stocks and Funds – Buying stock in a gold mining firm or buying into a mutual fund that invests in gold bullion is a common way to invest in gold. Most brokerage firms buy and sell these financial instruments. Gold stocks and mutual funds may offer more liquidity than actual gold, and there's no need for an investor to store or protect gold investments purchased in this form. That said, any gold stock or mutual fund investment may carry inherent risk and may drop in value regardless of the price of gold.

Gold stocks and funds should only be purchased from licensed commodity brokers. You can check the registration status and disciplinary history of any futures firm or broker by contacting the National Futures Association (NFA – www.nfa.futures.org).

Bullion and Bullion Coins – Bullion is a bulk quantity of precious metal, usually gold, platinum, or silver, assessed by weight and typically cast as ingots or bars. Dealers and some banks and brokerages sell bullion. Bullion coins are struck from precious metal – usually gold, platinum, or silver – and kept as an investment. They are not used in daily commerce. The value of bullion coins is determined mostly by their precious metals content rather than by rarity and condition. Prices may change throughout the day, depending on the prices for precious metals in the world markets. Coin dealers and some banks, brokerage firms, and precious metal dealers buy and sell bullion coins. The U.S. Mint has produced gold and silver bullion coins for investment purposes since 1986 and began producing platinum bullion coins in 1997. The U.S. Mint guarantees the precious metal weight, content, and purity of the coins they produce.

Collectible Coins – These coins have some historic or aesthetic value to coin collectors. Most collectible coins have a market value that exceeds their face value or their metal content. This collectible value is often called numismatic value. The coin dealers who sell collectible coins often have valuable coins graded by professional services, but grading can be subjective.

Facts About Buying Gold

Regardless of the form of gold you may invest in, consider these universal truths:

- The price of gold fluctuates over time. There is no guarantee that gold will increase – or even maintain – its value.
- The prices coin dealers, banks, brokerage firms, and precious metals dealers charge for gold products, like bullion and coins, are almost always higher than the value of the gold the products contain. So it's wise to compare prices before making a purchase.
- Some sellers say that the government may confiscate gold. Others say that "reportable" transactions lead to confiscation. Yet other sellers claim that modern bullion coins produced by the U.S. Mint are subject to confiscation while historic or collectible coins aren't. These claims sometimes lead people to buy historic coins at prices

that exceed their value. No current federal law or Treasury Department regulation supports any of these claims.

Investigate Before You Invest

Whether you are buying gold stocks and funds, bullion and bullion coins, or collectible coins, the FTC says do your homework first:

- If you are buying bullion coins or collectible coins, ask for the coin's melt value – the basic intrinsic bullion value of a coin if it were melted and sold. The melt value for virtually all bullion coins and collectible coins is widely available.
- Consult with a reputable dealer or financial advisor you trust who has specialized knowledge.
- Get an independent appraisal of the specific gold product you're considering. The seller's appraisal might be inflated.
- Consider additional costs. You may need to buy insurance, a safe deposit box, or rent offsite storage to safeguard bullion. These costs will cut into the investment potential of bullion.
- Some sellers deliver bullion or bars to a secured facility rather than to a consumer. When you buy metals without taking delivery, take extra precautions to ensure that the metal exists, is of the quality described, and is properly insured.
- Walk away from sales pitches that minimize risk or sales representatives who claim that risk disclosures are mere formalities. Reputable sales reps are upfront about the risk of particular investments. Always get a receipt for your transaction.
- Refuse to "act now." Any sales pitch that urges you to buy immediately is a signal to walk away and hold on to your money.
- Check out the seller by entering the company's name in a search engine online. Read about other people's experiences with the company. Try to communicate offline if possible to clarify any details. In addition, contact your state Attorney General (www.naag.org) and local consumer protection agency (www.consumeraction.gov). This kind of research is prudent, although it isn't fool-proof: it may be too soon for someone to

realize they've been defrauded or to have lodged a complaint with the authorities.

A Word About Endorsements

Promoters often use celebrities and high-profile personalities to tout their products. When someone says, "Invest in or buy gold with company ABC," think about what they're getting out of the deal. The fact is, many endorsers are paid by the company behind the product.

For More Information

Read these publications from the FTC at ftc.gov for more information and guidance about investing in particular gold products:

- *Investing in Bullion and Bullion Coins*
- *Investing in Collectible Coins*

Check these websites for additional information:

- Commodity Futures Trading Commission – www.cftc.gov
- U.S. Mint – www.usmint.gov
- U.S. Securities and Exchange Commission – www.sec.gov and www.investor.gov
- American Numismatic Association – www.money.org
- National Futures Association – www.nfa.futures.org
- World Gold Council – www.gold.org

The FTC works to prevent fraudulent, deceptive and unfair business practices in the marketplace and to provide information to help consumers spot, stop and avoid them. To file a complaint or get free information on consumer issues, visit ftc.gov or call toll-free, 1-877-FTC-HELP (1-877-382-4357); TTY: 1-866-653-4261. Watch a video, How to File a Complaint, at ftc.gov/video to learn more. The FTC enters consumer complaints into the Consumer Sentinel Network, a secure online database and investigative tool used by hundreds of civil and criminal law enforcement agencies in the U.S. and abroad.

Investing In Bullion and Bullion Coins

Read more in this Series:

- *Investing in Gold? What's the Rush?*
- *Investing in Collectible Coins*

If you're thinking about investing in bullion or bullion coins, the Federal Trade Commission (FTC), the nation's consumer protection agency, says your best bet is to research your options and get smart. Being uninformed can have serious consequences.

Bullion is a bulk quantity of precious metal, usually gold or silver, assessed by weight, typically cast as ingots or bars, and sold by major banks and dealers. You also can buy bullion as coins.

Bullion coins are minted from precious metal, usually gold or silver, and bought for investment purposes from major banks, coin dealers, brokerage firms, and precious metal dealers. Their value is based on their gold or silver bullion content. Prices fluctuate daily, depending on the price of gold and silver in the world markets. Perhaps the best-known bullion coins are the American Gold Eagle, the Canadian Maple Leaf, the Australian Gold Nugget, and the South African Krugerrand.

The U.S. Mint has produced gold, silver and platinum bullion coins since 1986, and guarantees their precious metal content. The Mint produces two types of bullion coins:

- *Proof bullion coins*, which are specially minted for collectors and usually sold in a protective display case directly by the Mint.
- *Uncirculated bullion coins*, which are minted for investment purposes and sold to a select number of authorized buyers based on the current market price (the spot price) for the precious metal plus a small premium charged by the Mint.

Foreign governments also mint coins, but they may not be produced to the same standards as U.S. coins and they aren't guaranteed by the U.S.

government. The value of foreign bullion coins depends primarily upon the coin's melt value – the basic intrinsic bullion value of a coin if it were melted and sold. A bullion coin's condition – its "grade" – isn't the most relevant factor in determining its price.

Investigate Before You Invest

Investing in bullion or bullion coins is a big decision. If you're thinking about it:

- Ask for the coin's melt value. The melt value for virtually all bullion coins and collectible coins is widely available.
- Consult with a reputable financial advisor you trust who has specialized investment knowledge. You may want to talk to other investors, too.
- Shop around. Most banks offer gold bullion, often at a lower markup than dealers. You also can enter the name of the coin into an online search engine to compare prices from other dealers.
- Get an independent appraisal of the specific asset you're considering. The seller's appraisal might be inflated.
- Consider additional costs associated with the investment. You may need to buy insurance or a safe deposit box, or you may need to rent offsite storage to safeguard your bullion. These costs will cut into the investment potential of bullion.
- Be wary of buying bullion or bars that won't be delivered to you, but rather to a "secured facility," by the seller or a third party. When you buy metals without taking delivery, you face the risk that the metal doesn't exist, isn't of the quality described, or isn't properly insured.
- Walk away from sales pitches that minimize risk and sales representatives who claim that written risk disclosures are just formalities required by the government, and therefore not necessary. Reputable sales reps are upfront about the risk of particular investments.
- Refuse to "act now," regardless of the consequences. Any sales pitch that urges you to buy immediately is a signal to walk away and keep your money in your pocket.

- Check out the company by entering its name in a search engine online. Read whether other people have something to say about their experiences with the company. Try to communicate offline if possible to clarify any details. In addition, contact your state Attorney General (www.naag.org) and local consumer protection agency (www.consumeraction.gov). Checking with these organizations in the communities where promoters are located is a good idea, but realize that it isn't fool-proof: it just may be too soon for someone to realize they've been defrauded or to have lodged a complaint with the authorities.
- Ask for a guarantee or certificate of authenticity for the bullion's precious metal content. Research the company behind the guarantee or certificate because certificates of 'authenticity' can be faked.

Tip-offs to Rip-offs

Bullion scams often involve false claim about content, rarity or value:

False Claims – Unscrupulous sellers often overprice their coins, lie about the bullion content, or try to pass off ordinary bullion coins as rare collectible coins. Some fraudulent dealers may even try to sell coins that aren't bullion coins at all. Others may try to sell bullion pieces with the same design as coins from the U.S. Mint, but in different sizes. Indeed, private mints issue coins that look like bullion coins minted by foreign governments, but may have little or no gold content. Your best defense is to study the market and choose your dealer carefully.

Leveraged Investment Scams – Leveraged investments are high-risk investments that can result in the loss of even more money than you originally invested. Typically, in a leveraged investment scam, a telemarketer or website will state that the price of metal is about to skyrocket and that you can make significant profits by making a small down payment for the metal, often as low as 20 percent. According to the marketer, by paying only 20 percent of the purchase price, you can get more metal than if you had to pay 100 percent of the purchase price.

In reality, you have borrowed money – as much as 80 percent of the purchase price of the metal – from a financial institution that claims it will hold the metal for you, and charge you monthly storage fees and interest charges. Rather than sending you a bill for those fees, the institution will reduce your equity in the investment. Once your equity falls below a certain level (for example, 15 percent of the purchase price), the financial institution will issue an "equity call," requiring you to pay additional money to bring your equity above the equity call level. If you can't pay or refuse to pay additional money, the lender will sell the metal to pay off your loan and send you a bill if the sale of the metal does not cover the amount you owe.

These investments are high-risk because you will receive an equity call if the price of the metal goes down, stays flat, or simply doesn't go up enough to offset the mounting storage and interest charges.

Glossary of Gold

Ask Price – The selling price a dealer offers.

Bid Price – The price a dealer pays for bullion or coins.

Bullion – Precious metals like platinum, gold or silver in the form of bars or other storage shapes. Bullion coins are made of these metals, too.

Collector Coin, Historic Coin, or Numismatic Coin – A coin whose value is based on rarity, demand, condition, and mintage; in fact, it may be worth more than its bullion value.

Melt Value – The basic intrinsic bullion value of a coin if it were melted and sold.

Premium – The amount by which the market value of a gold coin or bar exceeds the actual value of its gold content. The seller can recover part of the premium at resale.

Spot Price – The current price in the physical market for immediate delivery of gold; sometimes called the cash price.

Spread – The difference between the buying price and the selling price.

Troy Ounce – The unit of weight for precious metals. One troy ounce equals 480 grains, 1.09711 ounces, or 31.103 grams.

Investing in Collectible Coins

Read more in this Series:

- *Investing in Gold? What's the Rush?*
- *Investing in Bullion and Bullion Coins*

If you're thinking about buying collectible coins as an investment, the Federal Trade Commission (FTC), the nation's consumer protection agency, has three words for you: research, research, research. In fact, the agency says, there isn't a potential investor around who can afford not to spend time researching the coins, the graders who assess them, and the dealers who sell them.

Collectible coins have some historic or aesthetic value to collectors. The value of many collectible coins exceeds their melt value because their precious metal content is so small. Coin collectors refer to this collectible value as numismatic value, and they say it is determined by factors like the type of coin, the year it was minted, the place it was minted, and its condition – or "grade."

Dealers who sell collectible coins often have valuable coins graded by professional services. A grader examines the coin's condition based on a set of criteria. Then the grader assigns it a numerical grade from one to 70, and places it in a plastic cover for protection. But factors like "overall appearance" and "eye appeal" are subjective, and the grade assigned to a particular coin can vary among dealers. What's more, fine distinctions between grades can mean big differences in the value or price of a coin. The difference of one grade in the same coin can mean the loss or gain of thousands of dollars in value. Subjectivity in grading means there is real inherent risk in coin investing.

Expect to hold your investment for at least 10 years before possibly realizing a profit. That's because dealers usually sell collectible coins at a markup. It's how they make their money. In addition, the market for numismatic coins may not be the same as the market for precious metals or bullion coins. It's possible that the price of gold can increase while the value of a numismatic coin decreases.

Investigate Before You Invest

If you're thinking of investing in collectible coins, take your time and get to know the subject.

- Ask for the coin's melt value – the basic intrinsic bullion value of a coin if it were melted and sold. The melt value for virtually all bullion coins and collectible coins is widely available.
- Read trade magazines to check the wholesale value of coins. Keep in mind that collectible coins generally sell for a premium or markup over the wholesale price so the dealer can make a profit. You can find up-to-date wholesale value listings in trade magazines, like the Coin Dealer Newsletter and Certified Coin Dealer Newsletter.
- Be clear on the commission or fees that the metals dealer or broker is charging.
- Examine coins in person. It's difficult, if not impossible, to make a practical decision about buying a particular coin based on a photo or a conversation with the seller.
- Ask about the coin's grade. If the coin has been professionally graded, check into the grading service. Is it independent from the dealer? What's its reputation in the industry? Two services commonly used by dealers are Professional Coin Grading Service (PCGS) and Numismatic Guaranty Corporation (NGC). If you suspect that a coin's grade is fake or has been modified, check out the serial number on the coin's case or the grading document. Most legitimate graders assign a serial number to each coin they grade so buyers can verify the grade independently. You can check the serial number online or on the phone.
- Get a second opinion about the grade and value of the coin you're considering as a double-check on the validity of the grade.
- Get a written copy of the return policy. Many reputable dealers offer a return period if you're not satisfied with your purchase. Fourteen days is typical.
- Ask about buy-back policies because they vary among dealers. Some may offer to buy back your coin if its condition is the same as when you bought it from them. Others will buy your coin, but

- charge you a commission fee. Still others may offer only a store credit.
- Consider the tax implications. The Internal Revenue Service classifies certain gold products as collectibles. Income from the sale of collectibles may be taxed at a higher rate than other investments. Visit www.irs.gov or consult a certified public accountant for more information.
- Check out any coin dealers in a search engine online. Read about other people's experiences. Try to communicate offline if possible to clarify any details. In addition, contact your state Attorney General (www.naag.org) and local consumer protection agency (www.consumeraction.gov). Checking with these organizations in the communities where promoters are located is a good idea, but realize that it isn't fool-proof: it just may be too soon for someone to realize they've been defrauded or to have lodged a complaint with the authorities.

Tip-Offs to Rip-Offs

Scams in collectible coins generally involve false claims about grading, current value or buy back options.

False Grading Claims – Unscrupulous sellers of collectible coins often inflate the grade of their coins. Some dealers grade their coins in-house or through less-than-reputable grading services. Others create counterfeit grading documents or place lower grade coins in cases labeled with a higher grade. Walk away from the purchase if the case appears to have been opened, if documents appear to have been altered, or if a dealer won't show you the grading documents or let you examine the coin case before you buy.

False Claims about Current Value – Some dealers grade their coins accurately, but overprice them or mislead their customers about their value. For example, a dealer may charge $5,000 for an accurately graded $10 Indian gold piece, even though the current retail value of the coin may be $1,750.

False Claims about Buy Back Options – Many sellers of collectible coins offer "buy back" options to give buyers a sense of security in their investment. Dishonest sellers fail to honor the option, or fail to disclose commissions and other fees they attach to the option. In these cases, you may find that your true options are to hold the collectible coins or sell them at a loss on the open market.

A lot of people find collecting gold coins as not only an incredibly interesting hobby but a fairly lucrative one as well! Over time, your collection will accrue value and parts of it can be sold if you desire. This way, you will have additional income for yourself later in life in addition to a fantastic collection of valuable coins.

1. Face To Face: Coin Collectors Know Best

The internet is home to a lot of gold coin dealers wherein you can meet all sorts of people from all over the world who are into both buying and selling gold coins. Of course, it is a rather convenient venue for you to be able to do your transactions. You must be extremely conscious, however, when it comes to dealing with other gold coin collectors that you will meet through the internet. While there are some real gold coin enthusiasts in the internet, there are also those people who are posing as gold coin collectors and are just looking to rip you off.

2. Why Gold Coins?

The history of gold coins dates as far back as 2,700 years ago. The first gold coins in the world were issued in Lydia around 640 B.C. certain internet websites will provide you with a lot of information about the history of gold coins.

As money, gold coins have been a convenient way for people to do their transactions. Gold was only used for coins that were considered of a higher value. As gold is not the most common ore, it became impractical for gold to be used in the common coin systems of all major countries. This means a collection of gold coins is extremely rare due to the fact that gold coins are no longer being produced.

3. Gold Coins for Investment

• Gold is sensible investment: all major countries use reserves of gold (such as Fort Knox) to maintain their national worth

- A highly convenient investment

- Physical gold is extremely stable in value

4. Commemorative Coins

When it comes to the commemorative gold coins, since gold is deemed as a highly valuable kind of metal, it is an obvious choice when it comes to making or producing special commemorative coins. In the past, there are sets of gold coins that were just issued to mark coronations as well as other important state events. A lot of financial reserves that are being held by banks are in the form of gold coins. Gold coins are a desired form of a reserved asset since gold coins are not really used for circulation anymore.

5. About Collectors

There are a lot of various gold coin sellers, buyers as well as collectors who are waiting to bid on the best kind of gold coins in the market most especially in the internet. For most gold coins that can be bought as well as sold at prices that are closely related to their intrinsic gold content. The most popular bullion gold coins are the krugerrands as well as the sovereigns.

For most gold coin collectors, there are the highly coveted rare gold coins and a lot of gold coin collectors are interested in these rare gold coins that they will offer high bids just to be able to get their hands on these.

A lot of people who are looking for things to collect are in real treat if ever they try out collecting gold coins most especially because gold coins can be bought in highly excellent and may be in even mint condition for only a relatively low premium over the gold coin's gold content. Also, since the coin is made from gold, it is highly unlikely that it will tarnish or even discolor.

If you are looking into collecting gold coins, first research the various gold coins that are available in the market today. Find out how much they are really worth due to their gold content, and then factor in any additional value to the coin for being rare. Always be on the lookout for fake coins, and have coins appraised by a gold coin expert to avoid large differences in price.

Courtesy of Gold Investment News

Gold is a priceless metal. Most of the investors buy gold due to its value. Buying and selling of gold is very easy and it provides liquidity of money. But before buying gold you should be learning the facts about how to buy gold. You should know various forms of gold and the testing methods used and the price of the metal. There are different forms of gold that you can buy from the market. You can buy gold coins, bars and jewelries. The price of the gold various according the quantity of the metal contained in these products.

You should know about the various testing methods used in checking the quality of the gold. You should know about the different types of testing kits available. There are electronic testing kits with microprocessors in them. There are acid based testing equipment. There are metal detectors. You can choose any of these to test the quality of the gold before buying the metal. You can even use the magnet to test the purity of the gold. If it is attracted by the magnet then it is not a pure gold because gold is not a magnetic substance.

The next fact is the price. You should keep a watch in the market about the price. Every day the rates of these precious metals fluctuate. So you have to keep your eyes open to grab the opportunity of buying gold when the price is slightly lower than the normal price. You should talk with the dealers and manufacturers of gold to know about the exact market price of these metals.

Try to find out various companies who will provide you about different facts about how to buy gold. They will tell you the tips related to buying gold. You can check several online forums for learning the facts related to how to buy gold. You can search various social networking sites in the Internet and search for experts. They are the persons who can help you to learn more about the different type's methods and practices associated with gold buying. You can even find books from where you can learn the facts related to gold buying. With proper information about the topic you can easily buy gold from the market without being cheated. Dedicate more time to learn about the facts. Check various sources for information and gather as much as you can from these sources.

Experienced buyers and would be buyers make some mistakes while purchasing gold. There are many things that generally influence the decision of gold buyers. Here are some common mistakes that gold buyers make. The first common mistake that they make is buying these precious metals without knowing much about them. You should know about the product very well before buying them. You should know what you are buying like bars, coins, bullions or numismatics. Then you should know about the market from where you will be buying them and from whom you will buy these products. You should get educated about the market, sales and the products before purchasing them.

There are so many companies in the market from whom you can get to know about the different types of products. They will tell you from where to buy these products and who can you contact and also the prices associated with these products. They will help you to become a proper buyer so that you can easily eliminate the mistakes. The next common mistake is procrastination. Yes it is a very common mistakes made by the buyers. It has been seen that some of has the habit of delaying things even it is not the right time to do so. Suppose the price of the precious metal has fallen a bit, most people will spend their time looking out for more details about the price rather than investing in the right time. By doing this they lose time and the offers available. You should try to avoid such kind of mistake.

Most of the gold buyers never take the help of the experts. It is not a good idea. You should always check with the experts to know more about the gold buying processes. You should try to know about the services that they offer to educate gold buyers. You should try to find out the experienced persons in this field. They will tell you about the different types of mistakes that you should avoid while purchasing gold from the market.

You should collect proper information about the different types of mistakes that gold buyers make while purchasing the metal. You should jot down these points and try to rectify them by taking suitable steps. You can search the Internet and read articles about this topic.

Check various online forums and discussions to avoid such mistakes while purchasing gold.

- **Courtesy of Samuel Awonusi**

Gold is appealing and also a precious metal that is a good investment. Right now gold is a hot commodity because gold production is slowing down around the world. Inflation and the uncertainty in other investments is driving the price of gold even higher. If you are interested in buying gold you have to decide what type of gold you want and for what reasons. You have to decide whether you are going to want to sell the gold or if you are buying gold strictly for personal enjoyment.

Gold is appealing and also a precious metal that is a good investment. Right now gold is a hot commodity because gold production is slowing down around the world. Inflation and the uncertainty in other investments is driving the price of gold even higher. If you are interested in buying gold you have to decide what type of gold you want and for what reasons. You have to decide whether you are going to want to sell the gold or if you are buying gold strictly for personal enjoyment.

If you want to buy gold strictly for your own enjoyment then you will probably want to look into buying gold jewelry or gold coins. Jewelry is the most readily available form of gold; however it is not the preferred choice if you are buying gold as an investment.

This is due to the fact that the resell value of gold jewelry is hardly ever as high as the original price you paid. Plus if you are trying to resell gold jewelry there are no guarantee that someone will like that type of jewelry as much as you do. You will have to also realize that if you sell gold jewelry you probably won't get back the money you spent to buy it. Gold coins are a better choice because they are uniform and their gold content and quality are guaranteed. Selling collectible gold coins is easier than trying to sell gold jewelry.

If you are looking to buy gold as an investment you want to make sure whatever you purchase it should be easy to guarantee the content and quality of the gold. For investment purposes you can choose gold bullion which comes in bars and coins or you can invest in gold stock.

Buying stock in a gold mining company is riskier than buying gold coins or gold bars. When you buy gold stock you are not actually buying gold. It a gamble because you are betting on the gold mine to produce more gold, sometime that isn't the case.

Depending on where you live will determine whether buying gold bars to resell will be profitable or not. If there is a high demand among jewelers who wish to use the gold bars to make jewelry, than you might be able to make a profit. One thing to keep in mind is gold bars are not guaranteed by the government for quality and quantity, but gold bullion is. Gold that is in bar form is an easier target for tampering. The gold bar could be a gold shell filled with a non-precious heavy metal.

Gold bullion is the best type of gold to buy for an investment. Another popular choice is gold coins. Now is the right time to buy gold as an investment. Gold bullion investment usually increases in a recession. If you are considering buying gold just make sure you are aware of all of your options. If you want to invest in gold, make sure you are aware of the advantages and disadvantages.

 - **Courtesy of Lawrence Reaves**

The Gold Report Interview

In this exclusive interview with *The Gold Report*, Louis James, Senior Editor of Doug Casey's International Spectator reiterates his conviction that the dollar is on death row with no one prepared to grant a stay of execution. Dismal as it is, this situation gives rise to increasingly positive prospects for gold and other commodities that may ultimately stand in as the world's reserve currency. And there are some pretty hot speculative prospects—Louis' "best of the best" —waiting in the wings for the market's next big leg down that he's been forecasting.

The Gold Report: The last time you sat down with The Gold Report, you spoke articulately and persuasively about a U.S. currency crisis of historical proportions. At that time you said, "The dollar is on death row." It's been 14 months since then, and the dollar's position seems even grimmer. Can't the U.S. government find a way to grant the pardon that would prevent the dollar's demise? Louis James: This is one of those times when you hate being right. The short answer is no. The slightly longer answer is that while some actions might help the dollar, those actions won't prevent pain in the near future and they aren't politically viable anyway. It would mean embracing the pain the market doles out to people who make bad decisions, and those in government won't want to do that. That's not just my supposition or theory. You can see they're doing the exact opposite of what needs to be done; they're creating more debt, more "bubbliness," if you will, which is exactly what got us into this situation in the first place.

Doesn't "embracing the pain" for bad decisions point to the financial markets as opposed to the government?

LJ: Yes and no. The people in financial institutions caught in the subprime mess, for example, took risks, and one could argue that they deserved what they got. But it was the government that mucked about with interest rates and rules, and made those risks look sensible. Truth be told, I think all of this is a multi-decade long problem, a series of bad decisions, misallocations and distortions by government intervention in the marketplace that has serious consequences.

Trying to put the pain of correction off longer only delays and exacerbates the inevitable. Look at graphs and charts of these deficits. Look at the latest Treasury auctions—another $80 billion this week. The U.S. government is on track for another trillion-dollar deficit year. Not a trillion-dollar budget, a trillion-dollar deficit. These numbers were unimaginable to most people just a couple years ago. But you borrow that much, you create that much new currency, and the consequences are, as the saying goes, "baked in the cake."

TGR: We already have this trillion-dollar bailout, though. What could be done going forward?

LJ: They could stop. They could let the market correct the mistakes. But as I say, it's politically not viable. Because to actually do what needs to be done—to stop borrowing, cut down on debt, start producing more than we consume, put our financial house in order—would mean embracing the pain. It works the same way on a micro level in the family: sometimes you have to embrace the discipline, downgrade your lifestyle, stop dining out so often, stop going to movies all the time. Don't spend more than you make. That's what the overall economy needs. It's really no different just because it's larger. But that's not politically viable. Nor is defaulting. Imagine the leader of the world's great superpower going on TV and saying, "Oops, sorry; we're not going to pay our debts." So the politicians are stuck doing things that sound good to the mass of voters but make things worse.

TGR: There's a lot of talk these days about being in recovery, we're seeing some good economic news coming out, and Warren Buffet just put a big bet on the U.S. by buying Burlington Northern (NYSE, Stock Forum). What do you see in the economy that they're missing?

LJ: Let's get to basics. None of the fundamental problems in the economy that caused the situation have been fixed. In fact, as we've just been discussing, the government's actions have exacerbated them hugely. So what are the grounds for being optimistic? I think politicians encourage people to forget the fundamental reality that a society, just like a family or an individual, needs to produce more than it consumes in order to get wealthier. (Well, there's war for plunder—or theft, on the personal level—but that causes a net loss of wealth overall.) Pundits confuse people with talk about confidence.

They say that with confidence restored, people will spend again, there will be jobs again, everything will get going again and we'll be fine. All we have to do is restore confidence. But it's not true; you can't buy groceries with confidence. It's a shell game, a distraction. Confidence comes and goes, ebbs and flows. But in reality, either people can pay for goods and services or they can't. Either their production exceeds consumption or it doesn't. That's the key. If production exceeds consumption, you save, you accumulate wealth that can be used to create new businesses, to build new things, to hire more people. That—capital pooling—is what gets an economy going.

TGR: How can you explain how the market continues to rally?

LJ: Well, as the saying goes: the market can remain irrational longer than you can remain solvent. I should say that we at Casey Research have been on the wrong side of the market the entire year, because we've looked at the fundamentals of the economic situation. We have seen a) no improvement and b) the government doing the opposite of what needs to be done for there to be improvement. So we've been cautious. We made money; we bought when we found picks that looked undervalued, and certainly our oft-repeated call to buy gold has worked out very well. So, we're okay; but we'd be a lot more okay if we had ignored all the fundamental evidence of where the economy is headed. It's kind of ironic. Had we jumped on the bandwagon and deployed cash more aggressively—not to say foolishly—we would have made a lot more money. Instead, we've been calling for more correction, and still are.

TGR: Are you looking for another leg down that's as significant as the first or just for a more typical market correction

LJ: Bearing in mind that it's a good thing to have a daily dose of humble pie, yes, our consensus is that there's a lot worse to come. We see another and bigger leg down. The dollar, in particular, is headed way lower. The government deficits and what's happening with the money creation is all very bearish, more serious than ever, and that's really bullish for gold—at least as long as it's priced in dollars. But other governments are behaving similarly, and that too is bullish for gold.

TGR: Just for gold?

LJ: Our mid- to longer-term view on base metals is actually quite bullish, as well. The growth coming in China and India over the next 10 years is a major factor. But another serious leg down would knock the stuffing out of anything to do with industry, including the base metals, at least for the short term.

TGR: You recently noted a paradox of investing in gold—that is you buy the physical gold for safety and you buy gold stocks for its risk. Can you explain that?

LJ: As we've been discussing, gold has excellent speculative potential right now because of the destruction of the dollar. If dollars lose 25%, 50% or even 75% of their current value in a few years, that's very bullish for gold. But if that happens, we'll have a lot of economic turmoil, which is the real reason to own gold. No matter what happens, gold is still going to be gold. It's the only financial asset that is not simultaneously someone else's liability. It is not a piece of paper; it's not a promise from somebody else. It's a physical thing you can hold in your hand, and if push comes to shove and you have to hop in your car and go down the street and buy food for your family, somebody will give you something for your gold because they recognize it and value it. In extremely volatile times, you want that security. Gold stocks are almost the polar oppositein terms of security. They are highly, highly speculative. Most gold companies don't have any gold; they are exploring for gold or developing projects that they hope will be economic. Only a few actually produce gold, and even the biggest producers are highly volatile, because the price of their product fluctuates constantly and strongly.

So does the price of the electricity they use to produce it. All kinds of things fluctuate so much that these businesses—even the biggest ones, Barrick GoldCorp. (NYSE:, Stock Forum; TSX: T.ABX, Stock Forum) and Newmont MiningCorp. (NYSE:NEM, Stock Forum; TSX: T.NEM, Stock Forum)—are so risky that traditional securities analyses, a la Graham & Dodd, just don't apply. This isn't investing; it's speculating. You want the wild fluctuations of the volatile commodities market to create opportunities for big wins.

TGR: And juniors would be even more speculative. Haven't you compared them to burning matches?

LJ: Most of them are explorers with no substantial assets. All they have is money in the bank (hopefully) and an obligation to spend it trying to discover something. If they do make a discovery, they go from having literally nothing but a geologist's dream to having something of measurable value.

The difference in valuation can be huge; this is how it's possible to get 10-baggers or even 50 times your money on one of these stocks. The odds in any case are quite long. Even when you find a gold prospect, going from having a gold anomaly to a producing mine of any size, even a small one, the odds are something like 1 in 300. If you're knowledgeable and put a lot of effort into it, you may improve those odds, but the odds remain long. This is where the burning match comes in. The company burns through its money in the hope of finding something of value before the fire hits its fingers.

TGR: But the rewards can be commensurate with that risk.

LJ: Absolutely. The juniors' very volatility provides the opportunity to have enormous wins. But you have to understand it's a high-risk proposition. You can apply intelligence to reduce the odds, and you can diversify your risk. Whether it's your overall speculative diversification, or whether it's within an area such as gold stocks, you don't just want to buy one company. It works best if you have a portfolio of companies.

TGR: Any other techniques for improving the odds?

LJ: You tilt the odds more on your favor by betting on trends. If you didn't know anything about markets, if you had no idea whether gold was likely to go up or down, if you just liked gold and wanted to throw darts at the board, that would be pretty much pure gambling. But we have all this evidence we've been talking about regarding the economy to support the idea that gold is going to go up. A rising tidetends to lift most ships. If you pick the most seaworthyvessels with the most experienced management at the helm, assets of value already in hand and so on, you can do better than those 300-to-1 odds.

TGR: How about helping us wade through some of those juniors that have better assets in hand and better management, some that you're telling investors to watch because you feel good about them?

LJ: Okay, but with a caveat emptor. With gold higher than $1,000 for some time now, the market has grown quite heated. In 2007 and 2008, before the jitters, the market was overvaluing a lot of companies, practically anything with "gold" in its name. Some of these companies didn't even have any assay holes drilled into their prospects; all they had were theories and hopes, and they were trading for tens of millions of dollars. Since last fall's crash, there's been quite a separation of wheat from chaff, and many of the companies that had nothing but theories or hopes have not recovered significantly.

But many of the companies with assets of potentially bankable value have had great recognition. Many have not only recovered but have soared to new highs. That's not a bad thing, but it means that the companies with the best potential are not particularly cheap. But as we saw last fall, gold wobbled and came back strongly and quickly, while the gold stocks took a huge hit and took months to come back. That will happen again in another market correction. So maybe these not-particularly-cheap companies are cheap in terms of where they could be a year or two from now, but if you buy heavily now, you're at considerable risk of flubbing the first half of the "Buy Low, Sell High" dictum. At $1,000 gold, maybe $1,100 gold, people are getting excited and their buying is pushing prices up. I think gold will go much higher, but I don't know that it won't go lower first. Those who are psychologically disposed to follow the herd—nobody wants to think they are, but be honest with yourself—have to ask themselves whether they have the intestinal fortitudeto resist selling if your shares drop strongly, for no company-specific reason, before the eventual payday.

Imagine a person who bought, say, in May 2008, when the market was near an interim top. You know how would they feel in October 2008, when it just kept falling and falling and didn't look like it was ever going to stop. Most investors think 5% to 10% is a big fluctuation. To see a stock drop 50% in short order is inconceivable to them; they panic when it keeps falling from there. It's very difficult for people to hold on and say, "This retreat is not justified—I'm not selling." Actually, the thing to do last October, November and December wasn't just to hold, but to buy. People who bought then made so much money it's not even funny.

TGR: So are you saying that smart money right now should stay in physical gold until some of the frothinesssubsides?

LJ: If you're psychologically predisposed to being nervous about your investment, and you know you'd have a hard time dealing with a drop of 30%, 40% in a month or two, maybe this is not a good time to be buying speculative gold stocks. That having been said, if you stick to quality companies, buy an initial slice of your ideal position now, and fill out the rest of your position at a lower average price if it fluctuates downward, and you preclude the possibility of missing out on a stock that takes off. But you have to believe in your picks strongly enough to see a sell-off as a buying opportunity. Our general recommendation right now is to focus on the best of the best. Everything in the International Speculator portfolio has resources drilled off that can be defined by one of the regulation-complaint categories or another. And it's all gold and silver right now.

TGR: Okay, with that big caveat on the table, what are some of the companies that have the resources and management that represent the best of the best?

LJ: Right. Well, we really like AuEx Ventures Inc. (TSX: T.XAU, Stock Forum), which may have Nevada's next low-cost gold mine at their Long Canyon project, joint-ventured with Fronteer Development Group (AMEX: FRG, Stock Forum, TSX: T.FRG, Stock Forum). It's got great metallurgy. It's got great mine construction and operation characteristics—there's a nice flat place to put the plant and it's near roads and power. The deposit starts right at the surface so they can mine it in a low-cost open pit. There have been a lot of positive drill results since the last resource estimate, so it's going to get bigger and confidence in the known ounces will increase. How much? Who knows? It could be 50%, or more—or less—but it will be significant. Long Canyon has a lot of positive characteristics, and it's just their main property. Another AuEx property right nearby Long Canyon is called West Pequop, a gold project being drilled off by Agnico-Eagle Mines (TSX: T.AEM, Stock Forum). There's no official resource estimate there yet, but there's been enough drill success that you know a resource is coming. AuEx has projects in Argentina and Spain where other companies are spending the high-risk money, looking for a discovery, so it looks very good. And in terms of a company that can survive—they've got money, they've got real assets, they've got great management. We're very confident this company will make it.

TGR: Who else might be among the best of the best?

LJ: International Tower Hill Mines Ltd. (AMEX: THM, Stock Forum; TSX: V.ITH, Stock Forum) has a huge gold resource in Alaska they're drilling off. It's not particularly high grade, but it's got good grade for an open pit, and it has a higher-grade core. And it keeps getting bigger and bigger. It's got a lot to prove before the project can be put into production, and it's trading near an all-time high, so you might say, "I don't want to buy now; that would be buying high." You'd be right to think that if there's a correction in December or January, this thing could come off quite significantly. It's huge; it's getting bigger; it has the right characteristics to keep going, but its early stage. But whatever happens in the short term, if the company is successful, the value they create will be much greater than what the company's trading for now. So you'd have to see it as cheap compared to where it looks headed, not where it's been—and go in confident that if it retreats (barring any specific company bad news, of course), you can average down or hold out for the eventual payday.

TGR: Any others you'd like to tell us about?

LJ: On a slightly more speculative note, Andina Minerals Inc. (TSX: V.ADM, Stock Forum) has a very large project in Chile, which is a good mining jurisdiction. It's not particular high grade and the market doesn't seem to understand this deposit very well, and so it's selling quite cheaply right now. We've not been able to find a fatal flaw or any strong reason why these ounces should be selling cheaply. There is a national park nearby, but not significantly nearer than the Refugio Mine, which got permitted. Going there and kicking the rocks ourselves to see if we can figure this out is on our to-do list, but from what we can tell so far, unless we've missed something, this company is undervalued. And not a lot of things are undervalued in today's market. Inter-Citic Minerals Inc. (TSX: T.ICI, Stock Forum) is an interesting one as well. The company has a significant gold resource and terrific exploration success. The company's Dachang project in Qinghai province, China, has yielded a very bullish preliminary economic assessment. The internal rate of return was well in excess of 40% and the net present value was four or five times what the market is giving the entire company. But when they released the study, the market gave them nothing for it, and I have to admit I'm not sure why. They did drop the grade of the deposit when they came out with a more rigorous resource estimate, which could be a contributing factor—but in doing that, they increased confidence in the quality of the model. One of the things I really like about Inter-Citic is the exceptionally high correlation—something like 90%—between samples from surface soil anomalies and the trenches. In other words, where there's a soil anomaly they've been able to dig through the dirt and find gold in the bedrock. Then they come along with the diamond-bit truth machine, and the drilling also has correlated in excess of 90% with trench results. And there are a lot of gold anomalies not yet tested. So it's a great exploration success story with a lot more potentially to come; there's a lot of gold at Dachang.

TGR: Have you kicked the rocks there?

LJ: I have. It's a very interesting place, near Tibet. It is a refractory deposit, which is more expensive to process, and it's at a significant elevation. It's in a very remote part of China, too, but road building is cheap there and there are no regulatory hurdles. In fact, they have something like a 30-year mining lease already, so there are reasons to be cautious about the economics, but they do have a positive study and seem undervalued.

TGR: Any others you're watching?

LJ: We like Royal Gold Inc. (NASDAQ: RGLD, Stock Forum; TSX: T.RGL, Stock Forum). Most companies languished for months after the crash last fall and started coming back in March or so. Royal Gold recovered almost immediately. The reason, I believe, is that it isn't an exploration company. It's not even a producing company. It's a royalty company, with insignificant operating costs. Because its revenue is very much tied to gold, Royal Gold snapped back very quickly last fall when gold snapped back. The company recently reported record revenues and some of its juiciest royalties are yet to come online. It's a leveraged bet on gold. If you're bullish on gold, you buy a stock like Royal Gold, stick it in a drawer, and forget about it until the top of the market.

TGR: Which could be several years away. Let's hope. Any silver companies on your list of favorites?

LJ: We still like Silver Standard Resources Inc. (NASDAQ:, Stock Forum), Silver Wheaton Corp. (NYSE: Stock Forum, TSX: T.SLW, Stock Forum) and Silvercorp Metals Inc. (TSX: T.SVM Stock Forum). Silver Wheaton is more of a royalty company than a producer, but all three have huge leverage to silver and huge attributable silver resources. Silver companies trade at even more ridiculous multiples than gold companies, and these are all up-and-coming stories. They're relatively expensive, too, but I can easily see them trading at much higher multiples a year from now. Being a royalty company, Silver Wheaton has no mining risk. It just has revenue from the silver by-product of other companies' mines. Silvercorp has a super high-grade mine that makes money in almost any market. Silver Standard is probably the riskiest of the three because it's only just gone into production. If they fail to produce economically, they'll get whacked. On the other hand, that adds more leverage. They have something like 1.7 billion ounces of silver, and the market is valuing most of those ounces in the same way as an advanced exploration company. If Silver Standard can prove that it can produce profitably, those ounces could be revalued substantially, and this stock could very easily see a higher multiple than the other two. Or not—but that's what speculation is about.

TGR: Silvercorp, which is in production now, still represents some upside. Is that because you're expecting the price of silver to have a higher multiplier than gold? Or is there something unique about Silvercorp?

LJ: Silvercorp has very large resources of a very high grade, resulting in highly profitable operations. It's an extraordinary find they have at the Ying Mine, their flagship operation. The average head grade is still well over a half a kiloof silver per ton—that's after mining dilution and everything that happens getting your ore out of the ground and to your processing facility. That's very good. The fundamentals are there for Silvercorp, limiting the downside risk. Before the crash, the company built a new mill that could triple its production—and then put it immediately on mothballs because it was completed at about the same time the market tanked. They wrote it off, so they took a hit—which was a great buying opportunity—but it creates a special situation now; if they can ramp up again and put it back into use now, it's basically a free mill and thus very bullish for their bottom line. In addition, because the whole project was so high-grade, Silvercorp was able to finance their mine building out of their exploration by-product. They were exploring by drifting (tunneling) along the mineralization, and were able to take the profit from that to pay for sinking shafts and digging more tunnels. They built their mine without a formal feasibility studyor formal proven or probable mining reserves. Very cool, but here's the thing: the project has matured to where Silvercorp can produce formal proven and probable mining reserves. That will change the game, because there are some institutional investors that cannot invest unless a company has P&P mining reserves. According tothe U.S. regs, those shady measured and indicated resources Canadians use don't even exist. According to the U.S. SEC, unless you have proven and probable mining reserves, you have nothing. So when Silvercorp can start reporting a very high-grade asset, it will change the dynamics of their market. On top of that, they're bringing a new mine into production. If silver prices remain high, they can easily triple their output. The average grade may go down, but the overall revenues will go way up. I see a lot of upside here, with many years of mine life left at the super high-grade Ying mine to minimize the downside. If worse comes to worst, they can still keep cranking cash out of Ying.

TGR: What else are you keeping your eyes on?

LJ: We've had a really good lithium play that we made a lot of money on, and also a really good win in a rare earth play. These are more speculative things; but I bring these up because there's a lot of interest in lithium now. It's become quite the flavor of the day, and it seems that all sorts of companies are discovering they have rare earth potential in their property portfolios. Many are changing their business plans to become rare earth or lithium companies. There are good fundamentals there for the longer term for both of these specialty metal areas, but valuations for companies in these sectors just went nuts this year. My main concern with some of these trendy metals is that you have a really hot sector with really big wins with some of the stocks, but the underlying commodity price hasn't actually changed much yet.

There's this idea that all these electric and hybrid cars are going to increase the demand for lithium and rare earths, and that's probably true. It's a reasonable speculation, but it's a multi-year idea, and the price of lithium has not really taken off yet, while some of the rare earths have actually dropped in price recently. Economic concentrations of it are not an everyday occurrence, but lithium is not a rare metal, either. There's plenty of lithium around, and the current producers have huge resources. I've heard that there were times when SQM (NYSE: SQM, Stock Forum) in Chile, a top lithium producer in the world, actually returned lithium to its Salar de Atacamabecause they were producing more of it than the market needed. So it might be that the existing lithium producers can turn on the spigots faster than we think and wipe out all these new companies. TGR: Can they go back and mine that back out when the lithium market goes crazy?

LJ: Absolutely. It's not really even mining. A salar is a salt lake. It's got water underneath, so the lithium is still in the water, in solution; they just pump it right back out again. That's what makes these salt brines so cheap as opposed to mining lithium out of hard rock. You pump it out into a big evaporation pan. The sun evaporates the water and concentrates the lithium for you. That does take two years, though; so, if they turn on the spigots now, it will be two years before they get more concentrated lithium.

TGR: So, there might be a short-term bubble between supply and demand.

LJ: There could be. But how much under-utilized capacity do they have now? How much can they ramp up? There's a lot of debate about these are questions. Companies have an incentive to hint that supply might be constrained so they get a better price. Experience in physics, economics and comprehensible technical writing all contribute to Louis James' popularity as senior editor of the International Speculator and Casey Investment Alert.

He is also the interviewer for the weekly free e-letter, Conversations with Casey. Fluent in English, Spanish and French—and conversantin German and Russian to boot—Louis regularly takes his skills on the road, checking out highly prospective geological targets and visiting with explorers and producers in the far corners of the globe.

DISCLOSURE:1) Karen Roche, of The Gold Report, conducted this interview. She personally and/or her family own none of the companies mentioned in this interview.2) The following companies mentioned in the interview are sponsors of The Gold Report: AuEx Ventures Inc. (TSX:XAU), Royal Gold Inc. (TSX:RGL, Nasdaq:RGLD), Inter-Citic Minerals Inc. (TSX:ICI) (ICI.TO)3) Louis James - I personally and/or my family own the following companies mentioned in this interview: None at this time. (But that's because I took profits and am looking to buy back in at lower prices. I believe in eating my own cooking.) I personally and/or my family am paid by the following companies mentioned in this interview: none.

Gold coins have gone up a great deal in value in the last couple of years and since they are now so expensive, there are a few things you should watch for when making your purchases. With the advent of the internet, you are not limited to the local coin dealer anymore.

Gold coins have gone up a great deal in value in the last couple of years and since they are now so expensive, there are a few things you should watch for when making your purchases. With the advent of the internet, you are not limited to the local coin dealer anymore. This can give you the opportunity to get better prices on many coins, but also may introduce a few more things for you to think about when buying your gold coins.

1. Whether you are buying from a bricks and mortar dealer or buying online through a website or and auction site like EBay, check the reliability of the dealer first. For a store, at least check with the local Better Business Bureau. If the dealer is a member of the Professional Numismatists Guild (PNG), that is a big plus. For an EBay auction, check the seller's feedback rating. If it's very low, or there are many negatives, think twice (and a third time) before spending a large sum with them. Even if the feedback seems good, look closer, some people will buy or sell a number of very inexpensive items to build up their ratings, then jump in selling big ticket items. On large ticket items, ask if the seller will agree to use Escrow.com. They act as a middleman in the transaction and the money doesn't pass to the seller until the buyer is satisfied with the item. There is a charge, which the buyer would be expected to pay, but its well worth it when big money is changing hands.

2. One of the biggest problems buying collectible gold coins is grading. Your idea of an MS65 may be different than the dealer's. Many coins have a huge gap in value between grades. Avoid the issue by buying only coins that have been graded by one of the third party grading services. Make sure that you only accept the major services (ANACS, NCG, PCGS, NCS, ICG) grading, there are some lesser known grading services whose grading may be suspect. You should also want the grading to have been done in the recent past. Grading standards have

changed over time and what was an MS65 five or ten years ago, might only be an MS63 or 64 today.

3. Make sure the seller has a return policy that will allow you a refund if you are not satisfied with the coin. This should apply to both on-line and off-line dealers. This is especially important if you are buying a non-certified coin. You want to have the option to return it if your grading service returns a lower grade than you bought it at.

4. Buy the scarcest coin in the best condition that you can afford. Many collectible gold coins sell near the melt price of gold because there are more than enough around to cover demand. This is especially true in the lower grades. When gold increases or decreases in value, these coins will follow by a like percentage. But the higher the grade, the lower the population and demand will push up the price rather than just following the price of gold.

5. Try to invest regularly. As with the stock market, it's very difficult to call the tops and bottoms of the coin market. Over the course of time, you will fare better by dollar cost averaging than investing a large amount at one time.

Why Buy Gold

Mark Walters

It's easy to answer the question, "Why buy gold?" U.S. consumers are seeing their buying power dwindle and unemployment rates rise as the government deploys crazy tactics in a hopeless effort to slow deflationary economic pressures.

If you follow the news you heard President Barack Obama publicly warn that the US economy was "very sick" and "the situation is worsening."

How low can interest rates go? Well, in December 2008, the Federal Reserve slashed rates for the tenth time since September 2007. They dropped from five and six percent to an almost panic level of zero percent.

At the same time Congress-approved Troubled Asset Relief Program (TARP) doled out $350 billion to frozen-up lending institutions, hoping to disintegrate the banks" hoarding spree.

According to a November 30, 2008 Los Angeles Times report, the Federal Reserve had, by that date, actually loaned, committed, and guaranteed amounts totaling over $8.5 trillion. Minimal fiscal improvements have surfaced from these government tactics. Subsequently in 2009, the US budget deficit will exceed $1 trillion while the national debt will pass $11 trillion.

This news is sending thinking investors into gold as they wait for an inflationary time bomb to drop . . . Consider this scenario:

The slowdown of the US economy is evidently cyclical, moving from less buying power to lost jobs and less demand for goods. To stimulate buying, the Federal Reserve has lowered interest rates dramatically to free up credit and stimulate purchasing. Resulting low bond yields will eventually cease to draw foreign investors, who fear the purchase of diluted dollars.

The Treasury will print more dollars to buy up bonds, diluting the dollar's value even more. A hyperinflation cocktail is about to be served.

That's reason enough to protect your buying power with gold, but there's more?

China and other Asian countries are still lending the US money and buying up its bonds, but to a lesser degree in past year. Their buying will continue only as long as consumers and businesses buy sizable amounts of Asian goods and services.

With bank credit lines frozen and unemployment rising dramatically, US consumer buying power continues its erosion as spending systematically decreases. Foreign investment holders may soon catch on to US inflation worries and sell off their dollar-denominated reserves, moving to more stable currencies. Some already have. Massive Treasury sell-offs could lead to dollar freefalls and interest rate spikes, then hyperinflation. The dollar would be worthless, wiping out American savings and retirement accounts in unprecedented amounts.

So why buy gold?

Buy gold as an investment. Buy gold as a hedge against inflation. Buy gold to preserve wealth.

Statistics show the only asset groups making gains in 2008 were Treasuries, corporate bonds, and gold.

Historically, the value of gold has risen with inflation, outperforming other investment vehicles during periods of economic turbulence. Even during hardy economic times, gold often finds its way into a prudent investor's portfolio.

Many leading economist find today's financial landscape comparable to that of the Great Depression-even Weimar Germany. Now is absolutely the time to begin thinking about moving assets to gold, before the dollar writes itself into history's books as the next great fiat currency collapse.

Are We Running Out Of Gold?

Production at existing mines is grinding down at the same time investor demand is climbing. A quick scan of last year's individual country production numbers shows declines right across the board except in China whose citizens snap up all they can. China, for the second year in a row is now the world's top gold producing country, easily passing perennial top producer South Africa.

Since we are running out of gold very quickly, all the gold that's left in the ground is extremely valuable. Who does the exploration and development of gold projects? Who then mines, owns and sells the gold? Gold mining companies.

Newmont's raising $1.2 billion. Freeport is raising $750 million. Kinross raised $400 million two weeks ago. Also two weeks ago Red Back raised about $150 million. Yamana just raised $135 million and borrowed $200 million to stick $335 million in the treasury. Late last year Agnico-Eagle got $300 million from selling some stock after borrowing $300 million in the early fall. These major gold mining companies are planning on raising production levels and increasing their reserves by acquisition of other gold producing companies and post discovery resource definition juniors.

Our gold producers are quickly becoming market darlings. This is happening right now because dropping prices makes mining, milling and G&A costs a lot cheaper. It directly affects their bottom line making them suddenly attractive to mainstream investors whose normal stocks with their pathetic earnings are a whole lot less attractive.

Of course this brings up the question "Why do main stream stocks look so bad?" The answer is the worsening economic conditions, which have no end in sight and that gold shines in. Because of the breakdown in the financial markets and poor economic conditions I believe it's extremely important that each and every one of us owns some gold and keeps it close at hand.

What about holding larger amounts of gold as an investment? Money is starting to flood into the gold sector and both gold and silver look like their going to rise significantly in price.

Warning, I'm not a licensed financial planner, a broker, an analyst, a geologist nor an economist. And I'm also not, as you successfully opinionated about in your e-mails concerning my last article, an English professor. I'm also not a doom and gloomer or a gold bug. I'm just an investor who believes precious metals are a good investment and safety net to get into right now.

I believe this to be true because owning physical gold is the ultimate store of wealth and it also acts as a safe haven in the current worsening by the day crisis. Fiat currencies have come and gone since time immemorial but gold has always retained its value and its purchasing power.

In this, the second article in a series of articles about gold (the first article Gold.....ready to rumble! was about why gold/silver now), I'll be discussing the easiest most convenient ways to buy the appropriate physical gold products to firstly act as a permanent social safety net that can be kept close at hand and secondly to purchase and store offshore gold as the one true safe haven store of value it is. This dual pronged approach to gold ownership is a strategy that risk-averse investors and savers wanting liquidity combined with low-costs as well as protection from financial market meltdown should consider.

Buy very small gold coins and bars

A supply of different size/value gold coins and smaller bars kept close to home is the best way to ease the mind and navigate through troubled times. Say things do go to hell and you need to buy food, water or medicines with your gold stash. Do you want to saw different sized chunks off your large gold bar every time, do you want to chop your one ounce gold coin in half or quarters for smaller purchases?

No, you don't, what I'm talking about is a stash of smaller bars and different denomination coins easily stored, transported, sold and traded. The slight premiums for buying these smaller sizes are more than offset by the convenience of having different products of different denominations when you need to use them. Hopefully you never will.

Bullion coins come in a range of sizes from as low as 1/25th of an ounce to one ounce. A good safety net stash of gold is a combination of coins, wafers and one-ounce bars.

The advantages of owning the smaller denomination coins/bars include:

1. Easy transportation. Slip a couple half or one-ounce gold coins into your pocket.

2. You can take a Canadian Maple Leaf, Australian Nugget or an American eagle into any coin store anywhere in the world and it'll be accepted. Everyone recognizes the value of gold; in wartime pilots are given gold so if they have to bail out over enemy territory they have a

bargaining tool to use with the locals to help them escape. Who hasn't heard of people fleeing from tyranny and with the help of gold crossing borders to freedom?

3. Coins/wafers/bars are easy to store.

4. If you want to sell or trade some of your gold its easy to do.

5. Gold is actually very easy to buy, look in the phone book for a dealer (Gold, Silver & Platinum Buyers & Sellers in my Yellow Pages) that's close, drive over and buy some, it really is that easy.

Purchasing gold for most Canadians is very easy and convenient. I walked into a Bank of Nova Scotia, sat down, looked over a product sheet and ordered, paid, got my gold less than three weeks later. No bank or dealer selling gold in your town? Go online and use Google, you'll find many companies selling the appropriate size and denomination products that will be the most use to you.

There have recently been some shortages in the more popular one-ounce gold coins but other smaller sizes are readily available as are the smaller bars. My personal preference is for the smaller one-ounce bars and wafers in gold and then the smaller denomination gold coins. As for silver I like bars up to 100 oz's.

Getting a secure storage place for your precious metal stash should not be difficult or expensive. Buy a good safe, and keep it out of sight.

So now that you've got some physical gold and silver close to hand, to get through any emergency, how do you go about purchasing larger amounts of gold for investment purposes? What about insurance, offshore storage, access and regular updates combined with ease of buying AND selling? Is there a way to purchase gold much cheaper than advertised?

I've done an extensive amount of research and found what I think is an excellent place to purchase gold and have it stored offshore. I like this company so much I opened up my own account and I've entered into an affiliate program with them. Their name is Bullion Vault.

http://www.bullionvault.com

Why would you want to store your gold offshore, in a foreign country? If a country is descending into chaos it's usually not the people who are stopped from crossing the border but cash, gold, silver and diamonds. In other words capital is stopped from leaving, you aren't.

But I'd bet you'd find it pretty hard to leave under any circumstances if all you worked for and saved for your whole life was going to stay behind and you were being forced to walk away with nothing. But if your gold is stored in, let's say London or Zurich, you would walk across that border because you know you can sell your gold and start again somewhere else.

Another consideration is the often talked about confiscation of gold by government. If your gold is in Zurich it is highly unlikely a foreign government could or would even try to make the Swiss force a custodian to repatriate bullion.

Here are a few other reasons anyone considering purchasing gold for an investment in these turbulent times should consider dealing with Bullion Vault.

-Over 11,000 people worldwide have now bought and stored more gold at Bullion Vault's three accredited professional bullion market vault's (London, Zurich or New York) than most of the world's Central Banks own.

-The professional market, one you are otherwise excluded from, only deals in what are known as Good Delivery bars. These bars are guaranteed 99.5% pure gold or better. To get the best price buying and selling your gold you need to deal in this market.

-A strict "chain of custody" is followed. Because the bars have never been in private hands and are always moved by accredited bullion couriers, gold bar integrity is always maintained. Not having to re-assay to check purity when sold means trading costs are kept low and the trade is done quickly and efficiently. Buying and selling costs, called round trip dealing costs, were as high as 20% for gold coins in 2008. At Bullion Vault you pay a maximum round trip cost of 1.6% and for larger customers you'll pay .04%

- Through Bullion Vault you get access to this professional market and lower gold prices.

- Your gold can be held in accredited market-approved vaults in either the U.S., Britain or Switzerland and can instantly be sold from one jurisdiction and bought in another.

- Bullion Vault storage charges are less then one tenth of what a retail bank will cost you and less than a third what a Gold ETF will charge you as an annual fee, insurance included.

- There's many more reasons to use Bullion Vault but the bottom line is gold is cheaper, there's less hassle buying and selling 24/7 and your gold is safely stored offshore.

So there you have it, a two pronged approach to using gold as it was always intended to be used, as a flight to safety in turbulent times and as a store of value that preserves your purchasing power and builds true generational wealth.

I believe there is opportunity in times of crisis, that the set of circumstances we find ourselves in are better than they have ever been for astute and courageous investors. Are you going to be part of the group that plans to take advantage of the tremendous opportunity being presented for extraordinary gains?

- courtesy of Rick Mills

Buying Gold

by Tom Dyson

"What if my bank account gets wiped out?" My friend has nightmares about a virus attack on the global computer network. He says terrorists are developing programs that will wipe out bank databases. Account records will vanish, he says, and no one will know who owns what or how much. It'll wreak havoc on the financial system.

I have different "financial wipe out" nightmares. I worry the federal government will run out of credit and won't be able to backstop the FDIC. They'll be hundreds of bank failures, like there were in the Great Depression. In my nightmare, I lose my savings in a bank collapse. Here's another bad dream: Inflation gets so bad, the Feds impose currency controls and then devalue the dollar. My money gets stuck in the United States... losing its value.

These fears are some of the reasons I'm building a stash of gold coins and why you should, too. Gold is real money. You can take the coins anywhere you want in the world, and they'll always have value. Gold coins are the ultimate "safe haven" insurance asset. And here's the bonus: Right now, there's no "opportunity cost" of owning gold. Usually, you're giving up the chance to earn interest on your cash when you buy gold. But now, the dollar is paying next to no interest. Yesterday morning, I had breakfast with one of the largest private gold bulliondealers in the world. His name is Michael Checkan. He runs a business called Asset Strategies International.

I asked Michael what gold coins he likes right now. Michael told me you should keep two things in mind when you buy gold coins. First, you want a good deal. He says you should buy the coins with the lowest premium to the international gold spot price you can find. Right now, there's an orderly marketin gold coins and you shouldn't pay more than a 5% premium to spot. As I write, gold is at around $1,060. So you shouldn't pay more than $1,113 an ounce for your coins.

Secondly, you should buy coins with the highest worldwide acceptability, so you'll have no problem selling them anywhere in the world. For example, Michael says Asians prefer 24-karat gold coins, but the American Eagle and the Krugerrand are only 22-karat gold. They aren't so popular in Asia.

He also says the South African Krugerrand, the British Sovereign, the Mexican Peso, and the Austrian Corona gold coins are "passéand not as popular worldwide anymore. You won't get such a good deal when you sell these. So which coins should you buy? Michael likes one-ounce Canadian Maple Leafcoins best. He also likes Australian Kangaroo one-ounce nuggetsand the new American Buffalo coin.

The national mints sell these coins to wholesalers at a 3% premium to spot gold. The wholesalers take another 0.5% and the retailer takes 1.5% in profit. So you pay a 5% premium to spot. (The Buffalo is a new coin and supply is still a bit tight. If you buy fewer than 10 coins, you may have to pay a 6% premium.) These coins are all 24-karat gold, they are all popular worldwide, and you can hold all three of these coins in your IRA

When you sell, you should expect to receive the spot gold price plus about 1%.

There's never been a more important time to own gold than right now, even if it's just a few gold coins. We're entering severe financial turbulence, and gold coins are the ultimate insurance. Canadian Maple Leafs, Aussie Kangaroos, and American Buffalos are the best coins to buy right now. In my next essay, I'll discuss what you should do with your gold coins once you've bought them.

Trust Issues in Buying Gold Coins

by Anders Johnson

Information is everywhere on how to buy gold coins but how do you know who to trust? There are different types of gold coins to invest in and before any money is paid it is best to do a good amount of research.

People looking to strengthen their portfolios are investing in precious metals, especially gold. But as this practice gains popularity, more companies form that claim to be experts on the subject.

The best way to start is by searching online. Surf the internet for blogs, articles and websites that give relevant information on how to buy gold coins. There are several key elements to finding a reputable company.

First check out how long the company has been around. Search through their website to determine when it was created and put into use and if you can't find the information just call them. If you speak with someone make sure you verify the validity of their response by checking with company's like the Better Business Bureau. Most accredited businesses will be registered with them and show a rating of customer satisfaction and quality of service.

Also, look around online for user reviews of the company. Typically, not finding anything is a positive sign. Companies with bad reputations will, very often, have bad remarks left about them on several websites. Again, research the validity of everything you find to ensure you have accurate information.

It also can't hurt to call around and speak with some of the industry experts that sell gold and other precious metals. This is a very competitive market and a good company will have a wealth of knowledge and current market information. A good gold dealer will also take the time to gain your trust and make sure you are completely satisfied with their service. If you find someone asking for money quickly and assertively, beware.

Once you find someone trustworthy and get all of the information you need, then it's time to start investing. With the vast amount of options out there it's important to invest in gold, or other precious metals, that will yield you the greatest returns and have the largest long term affect.

Typically, it is recommended to hold on to coins and bullion for a minimum of 3-5 years in order to gain the most profitable returns. Rare coins, also called ?numismatic? coins tend to carry a higher spread, which is the difference between the cost to buy and sell, and to overcome these spreads and maximize potential profit, it is best to hold on to these for anywhere from 5-10 years.

For the best resources on how to buy gold coins just visit the internet where you can find current gold prices, information about rare coins and what is the best option for you. Dealing with a verified online dealer will give you the insight you need to be a successful precious metals investor and get you on the right path to financial security.

"When the dollar collapses, the best place for your money is with you, in the form of gold and silver coins." - **gold and silver dealer - Kal Gronvall**

You want numismatic American gold and silver in the lightly circulated condition, strictly for wealth preservation. Avoid companies that try to sell you bullion, or mint-state coins, or certificates in mining companies.

You want easily exchanged coins you can use as barter and money when the dollar collapses.

Use gold for wealth building, silver for barter.

Silver is what you use for barter, because silver is a small denominated coin that you can use on a day-to-day basis to get the things you need.

First of all, these silver coins have to be United States coins minted prior to 1964, when they were 90% silver. After 1964 they were nothing more than a copper sandwich with a little "chrome" on the top.

Gold, and How to Avoid the Scams in the Coin Industry

by Kal Gronvall

Introduction

One of the least understood concepts or commodities in our Western society is gold and precious metals. In almost every country in the world gold is revered, prized, and sought after. Throughout history, a king's wealth was measured in the amount of gold in his storehouse or treasury. Look at the Asian countries, or India. A person's wealth is measured in terms of how much gold he or she possesses. Central banks around the world hold tons of gold in their vaults as a backing for their paper currency. The Euro is currently backed by 15% in gold, and they are talking about possibly increasing it to 30%. The Federal Reserve has tons of gold in its vaults. But of course, that is not government gold, it is private gold. Gold has maintained its purchasing power throughout its 5,000-year track record, as the world's only monetary metal. Gold is financial security. For years, portfolio managers have recommended a minimum of 10% to 20% of one's total net worth in gold as a hedge against inflation or as a safety net in the event that our paper money system collapses.

But why don't we hear anything positive about gold in the media? Why is it almost impossible to get any information about gold? Is there a conspiracy to withhold this information from the American public? Why is it important to own gold? Who should own gold? What kind of gold is best for me? What is the best place to store gold? How can I educate myself about gold and gold companies so I don't get burned? Are there some general principles on how to buy gold? How can I avoid the scams or rip-off techniques of unscrupulous coin companies? Which companies are the worst scam artists? If you've been scammed by a coin company, is there any recourse? We will be answering all these questions and more in this paper. We will also tell a few tragic stories of people who have fallen into the hands of these gold company charlatans.

Understanding Gold, Greenspan, and Control

In order to get a handle on the gold market we need to understand a few basic principles about gold. Gold is the money of the Scriptures and, consequently, has been financial security for over 5,000 years. Consider the words of one of the most powerful men in our country, Alan Greenspan, the former Chairman of the Federal Reserve. Most people don't know this, but in the 1960's and '70's Greenspan was the biggest gold bug in the country. He was always espousing the gold standard and the value of holding gold over fiat money.

Here are a few selected quotes about gold from Alan Greenspan, "You always have to ask the question why is it that central banks hold so much gold which earns them no interest and which costs them money to store. The answer is obvious: they consider it of significant value, and indeed they consider it the ultimate means of payment, one which does not require any form of endorsement." "Deficit spending is simply a scheme for the 'hidden' confiscation of wealth. Gold stands in the way of this insidious process. It stands as a protector of property rights."

So why don't we hear good things about gold like this in the media? Is it a conspiracy to hide or cover up or withhold this information from us? Could the government possibly have other motives? Is there a reason they don't want us to own gold? A possible answer to that question came from Thomas Jefferson, who years ago said, "If you can control the currency of a nation you can control its people." Listen to the attitude of Baron Nathan Mayer de Rothschild. In a quote from a book *The Secrets of the Federal Reserve*, by Eustace Mullins, Chapter 5, The House of Rothschild, he said "I care not what puppet is placed upon the throne of England to rule the Empire on which the sun never sets. The man that <u>controls</u> Britain's money supply <u>controls</u> the British Empire, and I <u>control</u> the British money supply." The big money people in this country who run the country behind the scenes know that gold is the world's only money. And if they can keep the common people out of gold then they can control them during economic crises.

Just how do <u>they control</u> the common people to keep them out of gold? We will be covering who <u>they</u> are very shortly. First, they suppress the price of gold. By keeping the price of gold down they make it appear to be worthless. Secondly, they use a reverse psychology campaign against gold in the media, saying, "What do you want gold for? It doesn't pay interest or dividends. It is a barbaric relic. It is a thing of the past. It will never be any good anymore." Americans are constantly bombarded by this negative propaganda against gold, and it has been very effective. The end result: most Americans don't own any gold, and don't want to own any gold.

So, what is their intent? It comes back to the word <u>control</u>. What happens in economic crises when our paper currency fails and the stock market collapses? People whose assets are all dollar denominated will lose everything. When that happens, they can tell you which bread line or soup line to stand in. People who have a good percentage of gold in their possession will become wealthy overnight. That means that they will have to talk to you then, because you will be one of them, and that's the last thing they want to do. So, at all costs, they want to keep you out of gold. Without gold you have no financial security for yourself or for your family.

Is Gold Manipulated?

Now that we have established that the powers-that-be have other motives towards us in regard to gold, let's consider a few of their tactics to accomplish this objective. Is the price of gold actually manipulated or is it just another one of those unfounded conspiracy theories? I have read many different things about the price of gold being manipulated by the central bankers. One of the most direct quotes comes from that book on *The Secrets of the Federal Reserve* by Eustace Mullins. Also in Chapter 5, it says, "All of them (the big bankers) maintain close relationships with the House of Rothschild, principally through the Rothschild control of international money markets through its manipulation of the price of gold. Each day, the world price of gold is set in the London office of N.M. Rothschild and Company."

Almost a decade ago I heard the truth about gold manipulation right from the horse's mouth himself. At that time I was working as a gold broker for a large coin company in Minneapolis. One day during the summer of 1998, the president of the Austrian Mint gave a speech to us brokers. The Austrian Mint mints the Austrian Philharmonic, one of the most beautiful and popular gold bullion coins in the world. In the middle of 1998, the fears about Y2K were intense, and Americans were buying a lot of gold. In fact, in 1998, Americans bought more gold than they did the previous 10 years combined, yet the price of gold kept falling. It didn't make any sense. At the end of his speech, one of the brokers made an observation and asked the president of the Austrian Mint a question. The broker said, "The demand for gold is severe, but the price of gold keeps coming down. We have heard that gold is manipulated. Is that true?" The president of the Austrian Mint paused a few seconds and said: "Yes, gold is manipulated. That's true. It has nothing to do with supply and demand. The price of gold is set every day by a handful of individuals among three central banks, the Federal Reserve, London, and Germany." Now we know who they are.

The Gold Rush of 1980 and Central Bank Strategy

As a little history about gold in America, we were on the gold standard from 1850 to 1933, and gold coins were legal tender in our country during that period of time. In 1933, Roosevelt confiscated gold. From 1933 to 1971, it was illegal for Americans to own gold. In 1971, it became legal again for Americans to own gold, but not much interest in gold was generated until 1980. In 1980, we were going through a period of double digit inflation and double digit interest rates. People panicked, and they fled into gold as security or a hedge against rampant inflation. Gold jumped from $325 an ounce to $850 an ounce in less than four months. Silver also rocketed to over $50 an ounce during that same period of time. Now ask yourself these questions: What were people doing in the midst of that economic crisis? Were they buying gold or selling it to make money? Ninety-nine percent of the people were buying it, not selling it. It didn't matter how much they had to pay for it. They just wanted some real money, some economic security.

Before 1980, gold used to be a barometer of the stock market. When the market was up, gold was down, and when the market was down, gold was up. After what happened to gold in 1980, the central bankers learned the hard way that they can't let gold be a barometer of the stock market anymore. So, now, the rule of thumb is, the more severe the economic situation right in front of us, the more they suppress the price of gold, keep it down, and bad-mouth it in the media. It is all a matter of <u>control</u>, and the central bankers have the power to control gold prices. But their power is limited. All we need is another economic crisis and a panic, and the common people will flee into gold again. When that happens, the central bankers will not be able to control the gold price any more, and it will go out of sight. In fact, I have been talking to gold analysts for almost 10 years, and they are all telling me the same thing. Gold has been suppressed and depressed for so long, and there is so much pressure on gold, that when it does break, it will jump $25 to $50 a time, and nobody will be able to stop it.

Cost to Get Gold Out of the Ground, and Goldman, Sachs' Gold Purchase

We are now poised on the edge of the next run into gold. Why do I say this? Because the central bankers virtually destroyed the gold mining industry from 1997 to the year 2000 by suppressing the price of gold so far down that most of the gold mines in the world were out-of-profit and had to close down. For example, the cost to get gold out of the ground is about $320 an ounce for over half the gold mines in the world. The break-even point for about 75% of the mines in the world is $275 an ounce. In August of 1999 gold hit $252 an oz., and at that point, almost 90% of the mines around the world were out-of-profit. As a result, most of the gold mines in the world were forced to close down during that time because they couldn't make a profit. Consequently, as a result of most of the mines closing, world production of gold in 2007 will be the lowest it has been since 1931, and when the next run on gold hits, the short supply will disappear immediately, and the price of gold will skyrocket.

How do I know this? Simply follow the big boys' lead and you can tell what is going to happen. They establish trends and manipulate the markets everywhere, just like the Fed controls the stock market. As an interesting aside, Alan Greenspan, in a 1996 speech he made in Belgium, came right out to say, "We (the Fed) get into the market any time we feel there is going to be a correction to hurt us." In fact, have you ever noticed that at the end of the day, if the market is down 100 or 200 points, that it usually rebounds and ends on a positive note, or with just a small loss? Well, that is the mode of operation of the Fed behind the scenes, stepping in to buy stocks, securities, treasuries, bonds, anything it wants just to shore up the market before the end of the day. They usually do it incognito through a brokerage firm like Goldman, Sachs, or Edward Jones, or Smith Barney.

Getting back to the big boys. I don't know how many people remember, but a number of years ago Warren Buffet, one of the wealthiest men in the world, bought 20% of the world's above-ground silver with 2% of his wealth. It was big news in the media. He bought the silver for speculation, of course, because of the nickel, cadmium, silver battery that was coming up. And the whole world heard about it. Why? Because silver is an industrial metal, and they don't care who hears about an industrial metal.

At the end of 1999, Goldman, Sachs & Co. made a big move into gold, but nobody knew about it. They wanted to keep it as quiet as possible. Most people don't know this, but the Director of Goldman, Sachs is Warren Buffet. In August, 1999, Goldman, Sachs bought $124 million worth of gold from the New York Mercantile Exchange warehouses, which was half the gold in the Exchange, and they took physical possession of it. The brief article in the *Los Angeles Times* went on to say that Goldman bought the gold because they anticipate a gold shortage in the future because of reduced mine output. How better to know what is going to happen than to watch the big boys' moves and imitate them in our own small way. A week later, Prudential Insurance bought $43 million worth of gold from the Exchange for a client, and they also took physical possession of it. Two things are significant here. First, the big boys are moving into commandeering above-ground gold. Secondly, and far more important, is the fact that they want to keep it as quiet as possible. Why? Because gold is the world's only monetary metal, and they don't want anyone to know that they are buying it. But this move into gold is far more significant than Buffet's buying the silver several years ago. That small article about the Goldman, Sachs gold purchase was found in the Business Briefs section of the *Los Angeles Times* on page 17 under the want ads. Now we'll take a look at some of the scams in the coin industry.

High MS Coins for Speculation – The Wrong Road for the Wrong Reasons

One of the two biggest scam techniques in the coin industry is the recommendation by unscrupulous coin shops for people to buy high mint state (MS) numismatic (having collector or antique value) coins for investment purposes. They tell you that these high, MS numismatic coins are a tremendous speculative investment. And when gold goes up in an economic crisis these high mint state coins will appreciate tremendously in value, and you will be able to sell them and make a lot of money. Well, that sounds all right on the surface, but when you examine the logic of it all, it is complete foolishness. Why? First of all, the only reason to buy gold is for wealth preservation, so that in an economic crisis you would have some real money in your possession when our fiat (false or paper) money system collapses, or we get into hyperinflation, or the stock market crashes. The very last thing you would ever want to do when our electronic and paper money system is collapsing is to sell your gold and turn it back into worthless paper money. This doesn't make sense at all, but that is what these coin companies are telling you to do.

The Two Independent Grading Firms – PCGS & NGC

Now we will take a look at some of the things you should know about grading and some of the scam tactics of coin companies. First, a little explanation about grading coins and the two independent grading firms is necessary. During the 1980 panic into gold, great numbers of people were buying gold as a hedge against inflation. As a result of that run on gold, many coin shops sprung up around the country. Every coin company graded its own coins in-house. Naturally, the temptation to over-grade the coins was hard to resist, and almost every coin shop was guilty of doing it. The coin grading system starts at the bottom of the ladder with VF for Very Fine, EF for Extra Fine, AU for Almost Uncirculated, MS60, for Mint State (MS)60, all the way through MS70.

The way it works is, the higher the number, or grade up the ladder, the better the condition of the coin, and the more premium you pay for it. Coin certification starts with MS61. Certification simply means that the coin has been professionally graded by an independent grading firm to guarantee its grade. A certified coin is graded, encapsulated in a clear plastic case to protect the quality of the coin, and stamped with the insignia of the independent grading firm which graded it. The problem in the coin industry in the early 80's was that every coin company was certifying its own coins. For example, a person could buy an MS65 $20 gold piece from one company for roughly $2,500, and take it across the street to another coin company. They would look at it, bad-mouth it, and say that it wasn't even an MS61, and offer you $850 for it, a $1,650 difference in price from the coin shop across the street. As you can imagine, this in-house grade inflation was bringing a lot of consternation and reproach to the coin industry, and everybody's credibility was suffering.

In-house grading continued until the mid-1980's, when two independent grading firms came into existence, Professional Coin Grading Service, or PCGS, and Numismatic Guaranty Corporation, or NGC. In order to standardize and stabilize grading in the coin industry these two grading firms would certify every coin MS61 and above. Once either PCGS or NGC grades a coin, then the person who bought it is guaranteed that grade anywhere in the country – no fights, no hassles, no questions asked. A specific rule to remember is: if you ever buy an MS61 or above coin, either PCGS or NGC must grade it. If it is not, don't buy it – the grade is not guaranteed.

Introduction to Price to Gold Ratio (PGR) Chart

Just to give you an idea of how these gold companies operate and why they sell what they do, I have prepared what I call the PGR Chart, or Price to Gold Ratio Chart. This chart is a rather simple way to view at a glance not only what coins these companies are trying to lure you into buying, but what is the actual cost of that particular coin per ounce. Once you are educated to know their tricks, and you are armed with that knowledge, you will be much less apt to fall into their smooth rhetorical traps and possibly lose you entire life's savings as many have. For the purpose of illustration, I have chosen the most common gold coins that most gold coin companies sell. I would say that over 90% of the old gold coins that are sold in this country are listed in this chart, that is, the old United States numismatic gold coins that were minted from 1850 to 1933. Probably the biggest reason these coins are marketed so heavily, as I have mentioned before, is because numismatic gold coins are considered antiques or collector items and have some protection from a confiscation.

But here is the purpose of the chart: to show you where the big money is for the coin companies. It is in the Certified Coins. Certified or "slabbed coins," start with Mint State 61 (MS61) and go all the way to MS70. The coins on this chart are often called numismatic, fractional gold coins because they contain only a fraction of an ounce of gold. And incidentally, as the chart indicates, the big, big, money is in these high Mint State, numismatic, fractional gold coins. For the purpose of the chart we will look at the contrast in price between the MS61 and the MS65.

PGR – Price to Gold Ratio – Chart

Gold Coin	Fract. of Oz. of Gold	Times Multpl	Cost MS61 + 25%	Cost/ Oz. MS61+ 25%	PGR MS 61+ 25%	Cost MS65 + 25%	Cost /Oz. MS65 + 25%	PGR MS65+ 25%
$2..5 Indian	1/8	8	$425	$3,400	5.7 - 1	$5,625	$45,000	75 - 1
$2.5 Liberty	1/8	8	$381	$3,050	5.1 - 1	$3,075	$24,600	41 - 1
$5 Indian	1/4	4	$788	$3,150	5.3 - 1	$21,375	$85,500	142 - 1
$ 5 Liberty	1/4	4	$282	$1,125	1.9 - 1	$3,875	$15,500	26 - 1

99

$10 Indian	1/2	2	$738	$1,475	2.5 - 1	$6,60 0	$13,20 0	22 - 1
$10 Liberty	1/2	2	$419	$838	1.4 - 1	$5,25 0	$10,5 00	18 - 1
$20 St. Gdns	1	1	$844	$844	1.4 - 1	$1,58 7	$1,58 7	2.6 - 1
$20 Liberty	1	1	$838	$838	1.4 - 1	$5,47 5	$5,47 5	9.1 - 1

Prices of coins based on spot gold at $600 per ounce.

Formulas

Cost of coin per ounce = Times Multiplier X Cost of Coin
Price to Gold Ratio (PGR) = Cost of coin per ounce, divided by spot gold ($600)

Terms and Symbols

MS61 = Mint State 61 - Certified Coin
MS65 = Mint State 65 - Certified Coin
MS61 Mint State Grade with 25% mark up
MS65 Mint State Grade with 25% mark up
Times Multp = Converting the fraction to Times Multiplier to arrive at cost per ounce
Fract. of Oz. of gold = Fraction of an Ounce of Gold

To learn how to use the chart, let's take one coin, a $2.5 Indian, for example, and follow it across the chart. First, the $2.5 Indian contains almost one-eighth (1/8) of an oz of gold (Fract. of Oz. of Gold, on the chart). Now, to determine the actual cost of that coin per ounce, just convert the fraction of an ounce of gold in the coin (i.e. 1/8 oz.) to its round number, the (Times Multp = Times Multiplier) which is 8, because it takes 8 of these 1/8 oz coins to equal an ounce. Then multiply 8 times the cost of the coin (MS61+ a 25% markup). I have used a 25% mark-up on these coins in the chart, because coin companies typically mark these coins up at a minimum of 25% all the way to over 100%. So, I am being rather conservative for the point of illustration. Now we arrive at the cost per ounce (Cost/Oz) for that MS61 $2.5 Indian is $3,400. Now, for the last step in the procedure, to arrive at the Price to Gold Ratio or PGR, divide the price per ounce for the coin, which is $3,400 by the spot price for gold that day, which is $600, and we get 5.7 to 1, or 5.7 – 1. In other words, by paying $425 for that 1/8 ounce, MS61 $2.5 Indian, the buyer paid 5.7 times the current spot gold price ($600) for that coin.

Shocking? Just wait. Let's look at the numbers for the MS65 $2.5 Indian. Going across the chart and repeating the process again, the MS65 Grade with a 25% mark up cost $5,625, then times 8 for the multiplier, = $45,000 per ounce for that coin. Now, take $45,000 and divide it by the spot gold price of $600 an ounce and we get a PGR of 75 to 1 or 75 – 1. And that MS65 $2.5 Indian is not the worst scam on the chart. The

MS65 $5 Indian costs $21,375 per coin with a cost per ounce of $85,000, divided by $600 spot, which yields a Price to Gold Ratio, PGR, of 142 – 1.

High MS Numismatic Coins and Counterfeiting

The price of the high mint state numismatic coins is not the only red flag flying in front of you if you are considering buying one of these expensive coins. **The other red flag is that these coins are easier to counterfeit than lower grade coins.** Why? **Because there are two basic ways to determine if a coin is counterfeited, by measuring its circumference and by weighing it.** The scary part of buying one of these coins is, that when they are graded, either by PCGS or by NGC, or in-house by a coin company, they encapsulate them in plastic, thereby eliminating the possibility of measuring the coin's circumference and its weight. If you find yourself the unfortunate victim of having bought one or more of these expensive MS coins, you will be faced with the stark reality of how to determine the coin's authenticity if there is no way to check either the coin's circumference or its weight? That's why there is big money in counterfeiting. Imagine some shysters taking an ounce of gold, adding some copper alloy and minting an MS65 $20 Liberty that they can sell to the unsuspecting public for $3,500 to $10,000. Not a bad profit when you consider that they have about $650 per coin in materials.

Now you might ask the question, "If the two independent grading firms grade every coin from MS61 and above, how can a counterfeit coin get passed them?" That's a good question. I'm not saying that these companies are dishonest, but I personally talked to a man many years ago whose brother works for one of these two firms. I won't mention the name of the firm for obvious reasons. One day one of the largest coin wholesalers in the country sent several old gold coins to his firm and told them to grade the coins MS65. The company, without grading the coins, obediently encapsulated them in their official plastic cases, certified them MS65, and sent them back.

Giving gold bullion coins a grade, like the gold American Eagle or the platinum American Eagle, is another scam technique that some gold bullion dealers use. The rule is that only old United States collector coins can be graded. Gold bullion coins do not have any collector value, and are, therefore, not worth a penny more than bullion value. It is a scam to grade them because it does not increase their value or make them a numismatic coin. A few years ago a lady sent me a list of the coins she had bought from a gold bullion dealer in Texas. She had bought two 1999 gold American Eagle sets, a $5 coin, a $10 coin, a $25 coin and a $50 coin. These coin sets were graded by one of the two independent grading firms. And each of these coins was in a plastic case. There were no grades on these coins, but they were in official plastic cases. **The amount of bullion gold among the four coin sets was 1.85 ounces, worth approximately $520 at that time. She paid $2,400 for the four coins, or $1,880 in premium for coins that had no numismatic value.** She also bought a one ounce, 1998 Platinum American Eagle from the same company, and it was graded MS69 and certified and encapsulated by one of these two firms. She paid twice what she needed to for the bullion platinum coin. The coin company had convinced her that it was a rare coin because it had been certified by one of these two firms. One of my suppliers explained to me how this scam works. Coin companies will send 10 or 20 coins of these bullion coins to these firms and tell them to pick the best four or five coins and put them in plastic cases and grade them at MS65 to MS69. These firms get about $20 a coin to do the dirty work, so it is a good money maker for everyone involved, except, of course, for the buyer.

The Churn and Burn

Another common scamming technique is called the churn and burn. If you have purchased some American numismatic gold coins in the mid-grades, Very Fine, Extra Fine, or Almost Uncirculated, which are the kind of gold coins you should have for wealth preservation, beware of companies that try to convert those coins into expensive, high MS numismatic gold coins. The process is called churning. They will tell you that the lightly circulated numismatic gold coins that you have will not be considered collector coins in a possible confiscation – the government will look at them as bullion and confiscate them. They then tell you that only the high MS coins, which are for collectors and speculators only, will be considered collector items in a confiscation. **They will then try to persuade you to convert or reposition those coins into investor coins. Don't ever do that.** One woman in Nebraska had 93 ounces of lightly circulated Extra Fine $20 Liberties. She had the right coins for wealth preservation. Then a very good "Christian company" got a hold of her on the phone and churned and burned. When these vultures were done with her, they had converted her 93 ounces of numismatic gold into 51 ounces of expensive, high MS numismatic gold coins. **She lost 42 ounces of gold, which, in an economic crisis, could amount to a tremendous fortune.**

A Remedy for the Churn and Burn

The unfortunate victims who were deceived into buying these high mint-state numismatic gold coins for $2,000 to $10,000 per coin, when the dollar fails, will have to break them out of their plastic cases and use them simply for their gold content. In that day, no one is going to even think about buying your expensive numismatic coins for two to three times what you paid for them. At that point you will know what that gold company or that gold broker has done to you, but it will be too late. Ninety-nine percent of the people who buy gold are not collectors. They are just common people who have converted some imaginary money or paper money into real money as a hedge against bad times. In fact, in my 10 years in the coins business I have only run into four or five actual coin collectors.

If you find yourself a victim of a company who has sold you the wrong coins for the wrong reasons, there is hope for you. For example, if you were talked into buying bullion gold coins, or foreign gold coins, or the real high mint-state numismaticcoins, usually MS64 or above, there is a remedy that will ease the pain a little. It is called conversion. It is called conversion because you convert something risky or overvalued into something that will benefit you in the long run.

Here is how it works. In the case of bullion coins, like the American Eagle bullion coin, the South African Kruggerand, the Canadian Maple Leaf or the Austrain Philharmonic, the pain or loss is minimal, depending upon the spot price of gold at which you bought these coins. **I simply take the dollar amount for the bullion coins when I buy them back from you and switch that dollar amount into numismatic gold or 90% silver, whichever the client prefers.** That way, no money changes hands, and I ship you your numismatic gold coins or the 90% silver coins after doing the conversion. If you have purchased foreign gold coins like the British Sovereigns, French Francs, Swiss Francs, German Marcs, or any other foreign gold coin, the pain of loss is a little greater. Why? Because the coin company who sold you these coins usually charges more premium per coin than if you had bought straight gold bullion coins. And, of course, they always lie and say that these foreign gold coins are private because they were minted prior to 1933.

The purpose of conversion is twofold. First, you want to remove yourself from an area of risk into an area of security. Second, you want to have more ounces of gold and silver than you had before. Most of the time I like to convert high mint-state numismatic coins into lower grade coins, always gaining total ounces of numismatic gold or silver for my client in the process. **Sometimes the benefit of conversion is great, and the numbers are staggering, so don't despair if you have been a victim.** As an example, one man bought 700 - MS65 Morgan silver dollars for $56 a piece for a total of $39,200. The broker who sold him these coins claimed that these Morgans were worth over $500 dollars a piece at one point in history, and they were sure to reach that pinnacle again. Each Morgan silver dollar contains .77 of an ounce of silver. To do the simple math, 700 coins times .77 of an ounce equals 544 ounces of private silver. Based on the dollar amount of the conversion of these 700 MS65 Morgan silver dollars into numismatic gold coins and 90% silver coins, my client now has a 55-pound bag of Walking Liberty Half Dollars which contains 715 ounces of silver, and 46 one-ounce XF (Extra Fine) $20 Liberties. Now, let's look down the road a little at the value of these coins when the dollar fails, and gold gets to $2,000 an ounce and silver $50 an ounce.

If he had held on to the 700 - MS65 Morgan silver dollars, he would have had $27,200 of value in his hand, or 544 ounces of silver times $50 per ounce. He would have lost $12,000 from his original investment of $39,200. After the conversion, however, he had 715 ounces of silver at $50 per ounce, or a total value of $35,750. He also had 46 ounces of gold at $2,000 per ounce, or $92,000 worth of value. Totaling the gold and silver together after the conversion, we come up with $127,750. Remember, his initial outlay was $39,200. As I said, sometimes the conversion numbers are staggering. **So, if you have bought the wrong coins for the wrong reasons, there just may be a happy ending for you.**

Going just one step backward. If that man, at the beginning, had taken that original $39,200 and bought XF (Extra Fine) $20 Liberties, he could have purchased 100 ounces of private gold. At $2,000 an ounce gold, his total would have been over $200,000, or over five times his initial purchase. Not bad if you are talking about profit potential.

The Wells Fargo Find

Another expensive trap to avoid is buying coins from the Wells Fargo Find. Why? Because these coins are for collectors or speculators only, not for people looking to preserve wealth. A number of years ago, according to the story, and everyone has a story to spin, 15 bags (1,000 coins per bag) of newly minted $20 St. Gaudens gold pieces (minted from 1908-1933), were found in a Wells Fargo bank in Colorado. Supposedly, these 15 bags of $20 St. Gaudens were found under a bunch of boxes in the bank vault. Apparently, they were put there and forgotten right after they were minted in 1933. All 15,000 of these coins had very little visible wear and were in pristine condition. The discovery of these coins became known as the Wells Fargo Find. Rumor has it that these coins were actually found in a bank in Brazil, but it always helps to spin the story a little to sell the product. The two independent grading firms, PCGS and NGC graded and certified all these coins at MS65, MS66, and MS67. Many coin shops around the country started selling these coins for $3,000 to $5,000 a piece, as extremely rare, one-of-a-kind collector items. In fact, now one gold coin company is selling these MS67 - $20 St. Gaudens for $10,000 a piece. **Whatever you do, don't buy one of these high-priced Wells Fargo Find coins.** They are a huge rip-off.

Foreign Gold Coins and False Claims

Another favorite scamming technique that coin shops use is claiming that old foreign gold coins are numismatic, non-confiscatible gold. As a little background, in the middle of 1998, when Y2K fears were running high, Americans were buying a lot of gold coins, fleeing into gold as financial security. Numismatic American gold coins were very hard to get, so most coin shops bought old foreign gold coins, like British Sovereigns, French Francs, German Marcs, Swiss Francs, etc., and made false claims about them. They claimed that these old foreign gold coins, because most of them were minted in the 1800's or early 1900's, were numismatic, and consequently, non-confiscatible. They claimed that because these coins were minted prior to 1934, **(which only applies to old American gold)** that they would be protected from a possible confiscation.

In reality, any foreign gold coin regardless of its age or condition is considered bullion in the eyes of our government, and is confiscatible. If the government confiscates gold bullion again, the payback is $50 an ounce for every ounce they take from you. What these coin companies do is to buy these coins at spot gold or "melt" price, make false claims about them, put huge premiums on them, and peddle them to the naïve public. As an example, before Y2K, a "very good Christian company" was selling a 40-coin survival package of Swedish Koronas and Finish Markkaas. One of the coins was a little under one-tenth ounce, and the other one was a little under one-quarter ounce. The owner of the coin company stated in the literature that the total ounces of gold in this 40-coin-package was 8.98 ounces. But when I added up the total weight of the 40 coins it came to 7.04 ounces, not 8.98 ounces. So, he lied about the total ounces. The total price of the 40-coin-package was $5,015, or $712.36 per ounce for confiscatible bullion gold. Quite a bargain, and that from a man who quotes Scripture all the time and claims to be a good Christian.

Beware the Bait-and-Switch Technique

The bait-and-switch technique is one of the favorite rip-off tactics of coin companies. How it works is simple. **Companies bait you through the door by offering incredibly low-ball prices and then try to switch you to high-end dollar items after they get you there.** As an example, about three years ago, I called a man named Vinney, and we worked out a deal for two, gold $20 Liberty Double Eagles. Vinney was excited about the deal. Then he saw an advertisement from a well-known coin company on the Rush Limbaugh Show advertising these same $20 Liberties for 1% above cost, which amounted to $80 per coin less than what our company was selling them for. Vinney was going to cancel our deal and go with the other company because their prices were so much better. I warned him that no company could stay in business selling product for 1% above cost, so they obviously had to have other motives. I told Vinney that when they get you on the phone they are going to try to switch you to these very rare, high-priced MS, numismatic coins, and I warned him not to buy them.

I waited a few days and called Vinney back to see what had happened. I said, "Vinney, what happened when they got you on the phone?" Vinney said, "Well, you were right. They tried to switch me to those high-priced MS, numismatic coins, but I was ready for them because you had warned me. I bought the coins they were advertising for 1% over cost." I chided, "Congratulations, Vinney, you got a good deal. Now, tell me, what are you going to buy from them on your next purchase?" Vinney replied rather sheepishly, "I'm not going to buy anything else from them. They tried to cheat me." I said, "Vinney, you got the picture."

A Gold IRA – Don't Go That Way

Another tactic to avoid is a gold IRA. Many gold bullion dealers will try to persuade you to roll over your regular IRA into a gold IRA. They make you believe that having a gold IRA is something special, that a gold IRA is a hedge against inflation. That simply is not true. **A gold IRA is like any other paper investment. It is a piece of paper stating that you have some gold stored somewhere.** Most of the time they try to get you to convert your IRA into American Eagle numismatic proof coins that they claim are non-confiscatible. The truth is that they receive huge premiums for American Eagle numismatic proof coins, and that is why they want you to convert your IRA into a gold IRA. They make a lot of money on the conversion.

In the first place, the only gold you can legally hold in your gold IRA is gold bullion, and American Eagle proofs are considered bullion. Look at the face value of any American Eagle. What is it? It is $50. Why? That is the confiscatible value of that coin regardless of what you paid for it. Therefore, **if you convert your regular IRA into a gold IRA, you end up being a three-time loser.** First, you lost the flexibility of your regular IRA. Secondly, you converted your money into bullion gold coins, which are confiscatible. Third, your gold is stored in a bank somewhere in the country so you cannot access it quickly.

Gold Storage and Safety Deposit Boxes

Another thing to watch out for is a coin company that will hold your gold for you. Never buy from a coin company that does that. That defeats the whole purpose of owning gold. You want it there with you when an economic crisis arrives. In the midst of chaos what are your chances of getting your gold if it is stored in a company half way across the country? So, once you own gold and silver coins, where do you store them? **It sounds kind of crude, but most of my clients bury them.** Here is a possible plan. First, get a 6" diameter PVC tube like the plumbers use and cut it in a 12" to 18" section. The amount of gold and silver you own will dictate the number of sections you need to cut. Next, get a couple plastic drain ends like the plumbers use and some waterproof silicone. The gold coins come in plastic flips, so put as many gold coins as you can in a Ziploc bag and zip the bag shut. The Ziploc bag provides a double water protection. If you have silver coins, wrap them up in like manner. If you have a lot of silver, you will need more than one section of 6" PVC pipe. Once you have your coins in the pipe, then put some crumpled up newspaper in the pipe for packing and for water absorption, and seal the plastic drain ends in place with waterproof silicone. **Now you are ready for the next stage, burying or hiding.**

If you live in the country or on a farm, burying is relatively simple. If you have out buildings or a wooded area, just pick a spot that you can remember easily and is easily accessible. There is no specific rule about how deep to bury the pipe, but you want to make it shallow enough so it is easy to dig it up if you need to leave in a hurry, but deep enough to deter a quick in-and-out coin grabber. If you live in town and have a yard, then you need to pick a spot, preferably as far away from the house as possible, so it would be harder for a would-be robber to find it. If you live in an apartment, then the choices are more limited. I asked one very astute old gentleman who was living in an apartment where he stored his gold. Without hesitating he retorted, "My ceiling beams are sagging." Other clients store their gold in hidden safes behind false walls, cement them in basement walls, hide them under a three-season porch or tuck them away carefully in a crawl space. Basically, let your imagination be your guide. **The next thing to do is to tell someone you can trust where you hid the coins, preferably the person who will be getting them when you pass on.**

The last thing to do, as one old-timer suggested, is to develop a ruse, a scheme to deter or fool a would-be robber. To do that, put a few dimes or half-dollars or silver dollars in a real secret place in your house. Meanwhile, 99.8% of your coins are somewhere else, out of harm's way. That way, if someone comes to rob you, and if they threaten you with bodily harm, with great reluctance you can take them to that secret place and show them the silver coins, and you tell them, of course, that that's all you have. At least that way they will be happy to get something of value, and they will probably leave in a hurry without harming you. **Most people who come to rob you are in a**

hurry, and they don't come with a shovel in one hand and a metal detector in the other.

One last thing not to do is to store your gold and silver in a safety deposit box in a bank. Why? Look at what Roosevelt did in 1933, when he confiscated gold. He declared a banking holiday and raided everyone's safety deposit boxes. In fact, I personally have talked to five or six people in the last 10 years who have had things missing from their safety deposit boxes. I also personally have talked to one old timer who lived through the 1933 confiscation, and he told me a true story about a wealthy friend of his who had a lot of valuables in his safety deposit box. After Roosevelt declared a two-day banking holiday, the man went to his bank about a week later to check on his valuables. When he opened his safety deposit box, which had contained $1.4 million worth of diamonds, precious stones, jewelry, and gold coins, it was empty. He asked the bank president what had happened to his valuables. The man played dumb, and said that he didn't know. The man walked out the door, went home and committed suicide.

How to Approach a Coin Company to Reveal Its Motives Toward You

How do you find a coin company who will treat you honestly and sincerely and put you into the kind of gold and silver that is best for your needs? The simplest way to determine its motives is to ask them an open-ended question. First of all, when you call a gold coin company, make up a little scenario about you being afraid of the stock market and have just liquidated $100,000 of your portfolio, and you want to put that money into gold. Then simply ask them what kind of gold they would recommend. Their answer to that question will tell you from where they are coming. If they recommend buying gold bullion for speculation and they don't warn you about a possible confiscation, they are not the company for you. If they recommend buying old foreign gold, claiming that these coins are numismatic and non-confiscatible, run the other way. If they recommend the high Mint State numismatic gold coins for speculation, hang up and try another company. If they try to talk you into converting your regular IRA into a gold IRA, dial the next number.

On the other hand, if they recommend buying numismatic American gold and silver in the lightly circulated condition, strictly for wealth preservation, then they are probably a company worth talking to. My experience has been that more than 90% of the gold coin companies out there will try to scam you and put you into coins that you don't need. As I have said before, the worst scam artists are the so-called Christian companies. I have a friend who once told me, "When you see someone approaching you with a Bible in one hand and a flag in another, run the other way." They come in sheep's clothing, but as Little Red Riding Hood discovered a little too late, "My, Grandma, what big teeth you have." Hopefully, with a little knowledge of the scam tactics in the coin industry, your plight won't be like hers.

Case Studies – Tragic Experiences with Scam Coin Companies

Now that we have learned a little about what to watch out for when you are dealing with a coin company, let's look at a few tragic experiences that people have had with different gold coin companies. All these stories are true. I have talked to these people on the phone, sometimes for hours and sometimes over a long period of time. I have changed their names for obvious reasons. Many innocent people have fallen victim to these con artists who call themselves gold coin dealers. It is not uncommon for people to have lost tens of thousands of dollars before these wolves were done devouring them. Very rarely was there any legal recourse . . . a happy ending. All of these experiences are sad and tragic. But they all have one common denominator: they make my blood boil.

Anita and the Two Wolves

First, there was Anita, a 78-year-old widow from Oregon. One day a broker from a gold coin company called her on the phone. This company stated that they were legitimate, being members of the American Numismatic Association (ANA), which is the largest non-profit numismatic organization in the world. But better yet, they claimed to be a "good Christian company," and told her that they hold prayer meetings every morning before they start their business day. Anita, being a Christian herself, was impressed with that testimony, and she consequently trusted them from that point on. That was her first mistake. They talked her into putting almost $50,000 in MS64 and MS65, $20 Liberties and $20 St. Gaudens, at an average price per coin of $4,500. She bought 11 coins. That company, by the way, grades their own high Mint State (MS) coins. They do not use PCGS or NGC.

A few months later, Anita got a call from another gold coin company, also claiming to be a "good Christian company." They didn't hold prayer meetings every morning, but the owner claimed to be a believer, and so Anita automatically trusted him also. They asked her if she had ever bought any gold from another company, and she replied that she had. They asked her about the name of the company and the kind of coins she bought. She naively told them. They asked the years and the grades of the coins, and she told them. Suddenly, the broker got excited and told Anita that five of those coins were very rare, numismatic gold coins and were much more valuable than what she had paid for them.

The broker told her that he knew a number of international numismatic dealers and he would "auction off" those coins at their next auction and send her the money. He assured her that she would make a lot of money on the deal. The broker told her to send the coins to their company so the numismatic dealers could see them before they bought them. So, she sent him the coins. Two days later, the broker called back and said that he had buyers for three more of her coins. She sent them also. She didn't hear anything for over a week, so she called to find out if they had sold her coins yet. The broker said he never received the coins and could not remember even talking to her. He asked her to send copies of her invoices on the coins, so she made duplicates and sent them to him. Another week went by and she heard nothing, so she called back, and the owner said that the broker was not with the company anymore, and he didn't have any records of that broker dealing with her. Anita then called the State Attorney General's office for help. Unfortunately, he couldn't do a thing. A true story!

David – Twice a Victim

David, a 69 year old retired truck driver, was concerned about Y2K and wanted some gold to preserve his wealth. He called a woman whom he had heard selling gold on the radio. The thing that impressed David about this woman was the fact that she was a preacher, and she seemed sincere. She told David that the high Mint State numismatic gold coins were the best thing to buy for wealth preservation, and he bought 95 of the MS64 $20 Liberties for a total of a little over $60,000. So, David had 95 ounces of numismatic, very expensive, gold.

About six months later David got a call from a young man at another gold coin company, posing as the boss's son. He convinced David that he had bought gold that was much too high-priced and persuaded him to convert those 95 - MS64s into old foreign gold coins that he claimed were numismatic and non-confiscatible. David now had 134 ounces of foreign bullion gold. Little did he know that he had been ripped-off two times until he called me. Fortunately, this is one of the few stories with somewhat of a happy ending. I converted his foreign bullion gold coins into 114 - $20 Liberties in the Extra Fine grade. He now has 114 ounces of private, inexpensive gold. He did lose money twice at the hands of these two wolves, but now he has 19 ounces more of private gold than before.

Melinda and the Bear

Melinda's husband died leaving her $300,000 worth of stocks. Melinda was 74 years old and lived by herself in a modest home in Florida. One day a man from a gold coin company called her, the same company, by the way, that Anita had dealt with before. Melinda also was a nice Christian lady and was also duped by the aura of dealing with a good Christian company. It didn't take her long to find out just how good and how Christian they were. All the investments Melinda had were that $300,000 in stocks. She had very little in the bank and she was living on Social Security. None of that mattered to the broker. Using high-pressure tactics and coercion, he badgered her into agreeing to buy 66 - $20 Liberties and St. Gaudens at an average price of $4,500 per coin. The total sale was only a few dollars under $300,000. After the broker got her to agree to the purchase on the phone, he put the "company attorney" on the line. The "company attorney" told Melinda that if she agreed verbally to the purchase over the phone that she was legally bound to send them a check for the full amount. She was so intimidated by the two of them that she agreed to the purchase over the phone.

I had been talking to Melinda previous to her conversation with the other company, and I called her the next day. She told me the whole story. I went off. I told her that in no way was she obligated to send them a check, that these were unscrupulous crooks who were just trying to pillage every last hard-earned cent out of her pocket. She sent me their literature and their quotes for the specific coins that she was supposed to buy from them. Right there in their literature it says that they do not use PCGS or NGC to grade their coins. **They say that grading by PCGS or NGC does not guarantee the grade or the quality of the coin.** So, they grade their own coins in-house. That means they can take any coin of any grade they want, put it in a $.75 plastic case, put their stamp on it, and sell it for $4,500. The small print also states that they will buy these coins back from you any time you want to sell them, but there is no guarantee that they will be able to find a buyer. And the best part is that it is all in the name of God. Needless to say, Melinda never sent her check to those wolves, and she was extremely thankful to me for saving her from their jaws.

Nancy Lost It All

One of my saddest moments involves a 63-year-old lady named Nancy. One day in the summer of 1998, Nancy heard me on the radio talking about Y2K. At the time I was working with another gold coin company. She called in to talk to me, but another broker lied to her and said I didn't work there anymore, and that he could help her. She said that she was afraid of Y2K and had taken $10,000 out of the stock market and wanted to buy some survival gold coins. She told him that was all the money she had. She had no savings, no other money anywhere. She told the broker that her husband was an alcoholic and he didn't work. She had two part time jobs just to try to make ends meet and was baby-sitting for her daughter-in-law periodically just to make a few extra dollars. The broker didn't regard any of that. He got her on both ends, on one end with some high-priced MS63 $10 Liberties, and on the other end with some foreign gold coins. He took every penny she had.

I want to emphasize one point. I would not have sold that woman even an ounce of silver, let alone any gold. She didn't have it to spend. I would have told her to keep her money. She was in no position to buy any gold or silver. In fact, I turn more people away than I try to sell, simply because I fear God and I have a conscience. Many people don't have enough money to take care of their own bills to say anything of buying gold, so I turn them away. On the other hand, if someone has a great deal of discretionary money that is not earmarked for anything, I am not bashful to recommend that they protect a good portion of it with the purchase of gold. I think by now, with these few case studies, you have a pretty good idea of some of the tactics these wolves use to shear their sheep - - - - you, the consuming public.

Risk and the Stock Market

Now, let's talk about investment risk and some logical reasons why you should protect your wealth with gold. People don't realize the risk they are taking with their investments, whether they are in the stock market, the banks, government bonds, securities, CDs, or annuities. The most popular sport in America today is the stock market. Everybody is trying to get rich quick, gambling his or her life savings in what I call the Wall Street Casino. **People also don't realize this, but 98% of the wealth in this country simply doesn't exist. It is an illusion. It is either a number on a piece of paper or a number on a computer chip.** Yet, more than half of all Americans are in the stock market, gambling with utter abandon with their futures. Why do I say that? Look at the risk people are taking by being in the market.

Did you know that 47% of the money in the stock market is borrowed money? People re-mortgage their homes at 125% to 135% market value and put the money in the market, thinking they can borrow their way to prosperity. People run their credit cards to the limit and put the money in the market. Each year for the past four years, personal bankruptcy in this country has set new records. **The word now is speculation.** Wall Street keeps telling us that the Dow is going to 15,000 and then on to 20,000 – eternal prosperity if you stay in the market. Americans are no longer saving for that 'rainy day' as they used to. And as far as the purchasing power of our dollar is concerned, based on the 1940-dollar, today's dollar purchases only five pennies on that 1940-dollar.

Take a look at the NASDAQ as another area of risk. The average NASDAQ company is 206 times earnings. What does that mean? Simply stated, it means that if a company has one million dollars in assets, and their stock is valued at $206 million, that company is 206 times earnings. It is like a game of musical chairs. There is one chair and 206 people. When the music stops there is only one winner. Look at America On-Line, (AOL). It is all air. They have absolutely no assets, but they are valued at over $100 billion. If AOL would suddenly collapse, how many people will find the chair?

Mutual Funds – the Ultimate Risk

Not too many people are aware of the risk involved in mutual funds. Mutual funds contain more than half the money in the stock market, comprised mostly of 401K retirement money. During the last 10 years I have spoken with a number of mutual fund managers who told me some very interesting things about the downside risk of mutual funds. Mutual funds are required to keep seven pennies on the dollar on deposit for withdrawals. But in actuality, **they only have three pennies on the dollar.** They are only one penny better than the banks, which have only two pennies on the dollar on deposit for withdrawals.

What Wall Street fears the most is a run on the mutual funds, because when that happens, the Fed won't be able to stop it, and the stock market will collapse. So, to protect themselves from a run on the mutual funds, mutual fund companies ask you to sign a Mutual Fund Risk Disclosure Statement when you purchase into a mutual fund.

There are two points in that disclosure statement that are very important. First, it states "Under the Investment Company Act of 1940, **mutual funds may 'redeem shares in kind'** (rule 18F-1). This means that under certain conditions a fund **may redeem shares or assets in other than cash,** such as debt equities held in the portfolio." Second, they say, "**Under certain crisis market conditions, the Security Exchange Commission (SEC) may allow mutual funds to suspend redemptions.**" What does all that mean? It means that if there is a run on the mutual funds, and if they just ran out of cash, they can pay you in 'kind' – that is, any other 'kind' of paper. And regardless of whatever kind of paper they give you, whether it is stocks, securities, bonds, or a combination of all of the above, if you want to make a dollar on it, you have to find a buyer on the street. That is the truth about mutual funds.

The Banks and the FDIC

The banks are another great risk. As I have mentioned before, the banks in this country only have two pennies on the dollar on deposit for withdrawals. As a contrast, in 1929, right before the stock market crashed, the banks had $.21 on the dollar. And you know how many people got their money then. But today, the risk of holding money in a bank is 10 times greater than it was in 1929, because of the two pennies on the dollar. But we don't have to worry about that because each savings account is insured for up to $100,000 by the Federal Deposit Insurance Corporation (FDIC). Right? That whole concept is also bogus, because the Federal Reserve is neither a government institution nor do they have any reserves. The Fed is in worse shape than the banks, having only less than two pennies ($.01.6) on the dollar on deposit for withdrawals. But again, the American public is duped into believing this financial mirage, and so nobody thinks anything about it. A person has to be totally naïve to believe that the Fed will give you $100,000 if the whole banking system suddenly shuts down.

Your Money Deposited in the Bank – Do You Realize What You Are Doing?

And if the banks were not enough risk, knowing what your chances are of getting anything at all when there is a run on the banks, consider what Article 43 has to say: Article 43, Senate Documents, 73rd Congress, 1st Session, March 9 – June 16, 1933. I will quote a couple sections in this article, entitled "Contracts Payable in Gold." On page 4 it states, ". . . the Supreme Court said . . .that is such case the law was well settled **that the depositor parts with title to his money and loans it to the bank.** And if that is not enough of a shocker that you give up the title of your money to the bank into which it is deposited, here the legal definition of a dollar just a few sentences later on page 5: "**The dollar, consisting of 25.8 grams of gold nine-tenths fine shall be the standard unit of value,** and all forms of money issued or coined by the United States shall be maintained at a parity of value with this standard, and it shall be the duty of the Secretary of the Treasury to maintain such parity." **"This has not been repealed."**

The public simply does not realize that by depositing money in the bank that you are giving up title or ownership to that money and are loaning it to the bank. That concept or law being on the books explains a lot of things I have heard from ex-stock brokers and ex-insurance agents over the years. Candidly, they have told me that when they were trained for their positions they are instructed that when a person invests money with a brokerage firm or an insurance company that the money then becomes the institution's money and it no longer belongs to the client. **Therefore, they are taught to use any method of "persuasion" necessary to keep that money behind their doors and not release it to the client.** These brokers or agents are taught to intimidate, coerce, lie, talk about diversification, threaten, or basically do anything and everything in their power to keep that money behind their doors. Hundreds of people through the years have told me their own horror stories of these broker/agent, Mafia, scare techniques.

And, furthermore, that paper with ink on it we call money is not real money anyway. It is fiat (false) money, not real money (gold). In contrast, we have a debt instrument called a Federal Reserve Note printed by the Federal Reserve, not gold coins issued by the Secretary of the Treasury of the United States. The only way out of this fiat-money paper trap is to convert as much of the paper that you don't want to lose into gold as soon as you can.

You Think You Own Something – Think Again

To continue on with Article 43, on page 9, it reads, "**The ultimate ownership of all property is in the State; individual so-called ownership is only by virtue of Government, i.e. law, amounting to [a] mere user; and use must be in accordance with and subordinate to the necessities of the State.**" Bottom line: it is the kindness of the State or our Government which allows us to live in our homes, drive our cars, conduct our business, buy whatever we want to buy, provided we abide by their rules. But do we own those things we think we own? Obviously not, according to Article 43. And if the Government doesn't like how we are taking care of their property, well, you fill in the blank. **That is why we need to seriously consider getting as much out of their system as we can while there is still time.**

Do you have a lot of "money" in the stock market? IRAs? Annuities? Mutual Funds? CDs? Money Markets? Treasury Bills? Cash? Do you have most of your equity tied up in your house or in real estate? How liquid are you, and how fast could you get your money out of whatever it is in if you needed to do it? Do you have a plan to exit the system quickly or is your "money" bogged down or tied up in their system under threat of severe penalties for early withdrawal and increased tax consequences if you get out all at one time? The Government's system, like a giant glue trap, ensnares most people, and once most people are in it, it is almost impossible to get out. And believe me, in all my years dealing with people entrapped by the system, nine out of 10 people I talk to are so intimidated by the system and the adverse consequences of exiting it that they just sit there frozen like a deer in the headlights or stuck like a mouse in a glue trap.

Risk and Retirement – Don't Mix Them

In my business I talk to a lot of retired people who worked very hard all their lives to accumulate a little wealth. Most older people are more conservative than my generation of baby boomers, who are caught up in speculation and get-rich-quick schemes. But somehow, Wall Street's influence has had a great affect on older people's minds.

With all the hype about speculation and borrowing your way to prosperity, older people have also been caught up to the idea of gambling with the wealth that has taken them a whole lifetime to accumulate. That kind of thinking is very dangerous, because in a total collapse of the system, they will have nothing to fall back on. Wall Street talks a lot about diversification as a way to protect your wealth, **but people fail to see that if everything you have is dollar denominated, then you are 100% at risk. If the whole fiat (false or paper) money system collapses, and you have nothing outside that system, you will be completely destroyed financially.**

That is why gold and silver are so important. **Physical gold stands by itself as a sentry outside the fiat money system, guarding all of your assets.** Gold has a 5,000-year track record of being the world's only real money. Gold is tangible. Gold is real. Gold is universal and international. A person can take his or her gold anywhere in the world and exchange it for currency, or goods, or services. **Gold is the only financial security in the world. Gold maintains its purchasing power.** You have probably heard the old adage, that in the year 1900 an ounce of gold would buy a good suit of men's clothes, and in 2007, an ounce of gold will buy a good suit of men's clothes. When our dollar fails, do you have anything to fall back on?

And that brings me back to retired people. **As people get older and are past the days of being able to earn a living, they should be thinking about preserving the wealth they have accumulated, not gambling or speculating with it. As you get older, most of your wealth should be in a form that is insulated from risk or outside the fiat or electronic money system.** It is not like a person who is 30 years old and goes through rough financial times. If you lose everything you can pull yourself up by the bootstraps and recover. When you get older that strength to recover is simply not there. Here is another way to look at investments and gold. All the standard investments today are dollar denominated, whether cash, CD's, Treasury bills, securities, annuities, stocks, mutual funds, or IRA's. When the dollar fails, all these dollar-denominated investments will be worthless. **Gold and silver, on the other hand, have a dollar value, but they are not dollar denominated.** And that is the big difference. You can't protect your electronic or paper investments, your dollar-denominated investments, with something that is dollar denominated. It is not possible. That is why it is so important to have gold and silver, **to convert some of your paper or electronic wealth into gold and silver and have it with you in case something unforeseen happens.**

How to Preserve an Inheritance, Insurance Settlement, or Real Estate Sale

Most of us during our lifetimes will inherit some money from our father or mother when they pass away. Or we may receive an insurance settlement as a result of an accident, or we may sell a piece of land or property. What is the best way to preserve that money? Many people get grandiose ideas about investing that money in the stock market, hoping to get rich quick, doubling or tripling their money in a short period of time. Although that might happen on very rare occasions, the usual scenario is disaster. The stark reality is that most times people who gamble that way become losers. **Too late, these people find themselves victims of Wall Street's persuasive, prosperity propaganda.**

Sadly to say, but I have talked with many individuals over the past four years who have made the wrong decision with the money they had suddenly acquired – they put it all in the stock market. And when the market drops they start losing what they had put in. Then the only solution becomes the glue trap – stay in the market until it "hopefully" comes back. And while they are waiting for it to come back, it continues to drop, and they incur even bigger losses.

For example, a number of years ago I talked to a 63-year-old lady who received an $80,000 inheritance from her mother when she passed away. The lady's husband dabbled in the stock market and convinced her to put all of it in the market. **After three months of the market dropping, her $80,000 was now $30,000.** The loss of that money made the lady physically sick because her mother had scrimped and saved all her life to accumulate it and now it was over half gone. She pleaded with her husband to get the money out before it was all gone, but he stiffened up and assured her that the market will come back eventually - - more Wall Street psychology.

Individuals who have money and want to keep it, look at the market as a game, another form of casino. If they have $50,000 to play with they might throw it into IBM stock or another blue-chip stock or high tech stock and leave it in there for a few days. If the stock makes a sudden spike upward they quickly pull it out and make a profit. The big money people only use their play money in the market. They are too smart to do otherwise because they know that the stock market game is fickle. **It is an illusion or a mirage, created to make losers out of the ignorant, naïve, or unsuspecting.**

Another man got $450,000 in blue-chip stocks from his father when he passed away. The market was coming down at the time, and his gut response was to pull it out immediately before he lost any of it. His smooth-talking broker, however, persuaded him to wait a couple weeks to see what would happen. After two weeks he had lost $20,000. Again, against his better judgment, his broker told him that the market correction was only temporary, and to leave it in there until it rebounded. The market continued to come down, and his stocks were only worth $385,000. **He still didn't learn his lesson. He was stuck in the Wall Street Casino glue trap.** He didn't want to get out and take the loss but stay in and recoup some of the money he had lost. But will that happen? – not likely. **The market is a game, and if you don't know the rules you better not play.**

The safest thing to do with an inheritance or a lump sum from the sale of a piece of property or an insurance settlement is to put it into gold and silver. That is the only sure way to preserve it. In the 10 years I have been in the coin industry I have dealt with many people who have done just that. The amazing thing about most of these people is that they thought of the idea themselves. I really did not have to coax them at all. Most of these people getting inheritances from their parents are older people, and their parents went through the Great Depression of the 1930's. They know the value of money and the value of gold. Their parents told them that gold is the world's only money, and it will always have value. One 67 year old lady got $100,000 from her mother when she passed away, and she put it all into gold and silver. **She told me after she got her gold and silver that she now has great peace of mind to know that that money can't disappear or vanish in a market collapse or when the dollar fails.** Another lady received a $60,000 inheritance from her mother. She also put it all into gold. Of course, I make sure with each of these individuals that they have plenty of other money on which to live, so they are not taking money they would need to live on to put into gold.

Another young couple got an insurance settlement of $250,000. The husband was only 35 years old and had been injured in a car accident. They decided to put $100,000 into gold and silver and use the rest to pay off debt. Another middle-aged couple got $100,000 from the husband's father when he passed away. So far, they have put $65,000 into gold and silver. Another man got $250,000 from his mother when she died. He paid off his house, and put $75,000 into gold and silver. And the list goes on. All these people today are excited about what they did, because they know that when our dollar collapses, gold and silver will go out of sight, and they will be wealthy overnight. Not that being wealthy is important to them. **The important thing is that they know that they have real financial security because they have gold.**

Who Should Buy Gold, Percentages, and a Lesson on How to Buy Gold

Who should buy gold and what percentage should you buy? Not everybody is in the financial place to buy gold. If you are living from paycheck to paycheck, then gold is not for you. If you have some discretionary money that is not earmarked for anything, then you should consider buying some gold and silver. If you are retired and you have wealth that you want to protect, you should buy gold. What percentage should you put into gold? **Generally, portfolio managers for years have recommended between 10% and 20% of your total net worth into the precious metals.** Why those percentages? To illustrate, let's look at a likely scenario. Suppose that your net worth, with your house, your property, and your investments is $250,000. If you had 20% of your net worth in gold you would have about $50,000 in gold. At today's spot gold price of $650, with that $50,000 you could buy about 70 ounces of slightly circulated, $20 Liberties. In the event that our dollar fails, gold will go out of sight. We could expect gold, as gold analysts are now saying, to get between $3,000 and $10,000 an ounce. Using the low figure of $3,000 an ounce for gold, times 70 ounces, equals $210,000. That's how gold protects all of your net worth, because it will multiply in value to cover all your dollar-denominated losses when our currency collapses.

So, if you are retired and have substantial wealth, the percentage you hold in gold should be higher. I like to put it this way: **Don't have anything in financial institutions that you can't afford to lose, and if you lose it, it shouldn't hurt you.** Or another way to say: Whatever you don't want to lose, put it into gold. And, another general recommendation is that, of the precious metals that you have in your possession, 90% should be in gold because that is your core of wealth, your compact store of value. And 10% should be in silver for barter. They each have their own purpose: gold is for wealth preservation and silver is for barter.

Here is a little lesson on how to buy gold. **There are two ways to buy gold: gold bullion and numismatic gold coins.** When most people think of gold bullion they think about the big bars of gold in Fort Knox. **The most common form of bullion today is the one ounce gold coins,** like the American Eagle, the Canadian Maple Leaf, the South African Kruggerand, the Austrian Philharmonic, the Mexican Pesos, the Chinese Panda, etc. These coins are all coins of the realm, but they have never been circulated as legal tender in any of these countries from which they came.

Also considered bullion are any foreign gold coins that have been legal tender in their respective countries, like the British Sovereign, the Swiss Franc, the French Franc, the Finish Markkaas, the German Marc, etc. These coins, regardless of their age or condition, are also considered bullion in the eyes of our government. Why? There are 49 countries around the world that allow their citizens to hold their own countries' numismatic gold and silver coins without fear of confiscation, if they are in good enough condition to be considered a collector item. It is a way to preserve the country's history in coin form. But they do not exempt another countries' old gold or silver coins, just their own. And America is no different. **In this country, we only exempt old American gold and old American silver, not foreign gold and silver.**

The biggest thing about bullion is that it is for speculators, people who buy it cheaply, and when gold goes up, they quickly sell it and make money. My clients are not speculators. <u>They are interested strictly in wealth preservation.</u> **The worst part about bullion, however, is that it is confiscatible.** The government can take it any time they want, **and they will pay you $50 an ounce in paper money for every ounce they take from you.** That is not the kind of risk I want to put my clients into, and that is not the kind of risk my clients want to take.

That is why I recommend the lightly circulated numismatic gold coins Now, these are the old $20 Liberties, $20 St. Gaudens, $10 Liberties, $5 Liberties, coins that were legal tender in our country from 1850 to 1933. And if they are in good enough condition to be considered a collector item, then they are considered numismatic gold, non-reportable, and non-confiscatible. Now, within the numismatic arena, there are two specific areas. One area I do not recommend and the other I do recommend. As I have already mentioned, **I do not recommend the real rare, high Mint State (MS) numismatic gold coins.** These high MS coins are for collectors only, not for people looking for wealth preservation. The difference in the price of a slightly circulated old gold coin and an MS65 to MS67 is between six and 25 times. So why would anybody want one of those coins? They are a huge rip-off. **And remember, the only thing rarer than a rare coin is a buyer for a rare coin.**

The area I do recommend is the numismatic gold coins in the lightly circulated grades, the Very Fine (VF), the Extra Fine (XF), and the Almost Uncirculated (AU). These coins have slight wear, but to the untrained eye they don't appear to have any wear at all. They are in beautiful condition. But because they have slight wear, the premium is more moderate than the high MS coins. And there is no reason to pay even a dollar more premium than you have to acquire numismatic gold coins. **The high MS coins and the lightly circulated numismatic gold coins are both considered collector items and are non-confiscatible, so why throw your money away on premium if you don't have to?**

Gold is for Preserving Wealth, and Silver is for Barter

As I have mentioned before many times in this paper, gold and silver serve two purposes. Gold is for preserving wealth, and silver is for barter. **Probably the most common question I am asked about the precious metals is how could a person use them in the event of a currency collapse?** People ask me, "How can I use my gold coins for barter when the time comes? Do I saw off an edge of the coin and use it that way? How will people know the value of gold and silver? The answers to these questions are relatively simple. No one knows exactly how things are going to unfold, but we could pose a very possible scenario.

Suppose that our dollar fails, and it will one of these days. When the dollar fails, gold and silver will go out of sight. People will flee into gold and silver again for financial security as they did in 1980, when we got into double-digit inflation and double-digit interest rates. Gold hit $850 an ounce and silver hit $50 an ounce in a short four-month period of time. When the next run on gold happens, gold will sky rocket past the 1980 high. Gold analysts are now saying, as I mentioned before, that because of the severe shortage of above-ground gold today, **that gold could easily climb to $2,000 and $10,000 an ounce, and silver could get to $50 to $100 per ounce.** I don't use these numbers to try to impress you but to illustrate a point. The whole idea behind owning gold and silver is that you will have some real money in your hand with which to buy the things you need when the dollar goes south.

Now to answer the question about how you could use your gold and silver for barter. First of all, gold is not for barter but for preserving wealth. **Gold will simply be too valuable per ounce to use for barter.** You can't take a one ounce gold piece, which could be worth $2,000 per ounce, down to the grocery store or get a tank of gas with it. It is not practical. Gold is something that you hang on to as your core of wealth. Later on, if things finally settle down, you can either convert your gold to currency, if and when our government prints another currency, or you could use it to buy bigger things like a house or a car or a piece of land.

As an interesting piece of history, in 1929, when the stock market crashed, land values plummeted 75% to 95%, and people with money were able to pick up houses or land for pennies on the dollar. The same thing will happen this time when our dollar fails and the market crashes. **The only thing different this time is that the money will be worthless, and with gold in your possession you will be able to pick up houses or land or bigger things for pennies on the dollar.** And, if you don't see a collapse of the dollar in your lifetime, simply pass on your gold quietly to your children before you leave. No muss, no fuss, no paper work, no government, and no probate. In fact, that is how the big boys, the ones who own the Federal Reserve, operate. They have converted about 80% of their personal wealth into gold, and they pass on their wealth to their children, and the government doesn't know a thing.

Silver for Barter

Now, getting back to the question about barter. **Silver is what you use for barter, because silver is a small denominated coin that you can use on a day-to-day basis to get the things you need.** Say, for example, in our scenario, that after the dollar collapses, silver gets to $50 an ounce. How would people know the value of a silver coin, whether it is a dime, quarter, half-dollar or silver dollar? First of all, these silver coins have to be United States coins minted prior to 1964, when they were 90% silver. After 1964 they were nothing more than a copper sandwich with a little "chrome" on the top.

If silver gets to $50 per ounce, all we have to know is how much actual silver is in the individual coin and we can calculate its value based on a $50 per ounce. For example, the Mercury Dime contains .07 of an ounce of silver, and if we multiply that times $50 an oz. for silver, it equals $3.50. If a loaf of bread is $3 or $4, you could buy a loaf of bread with that Mercury Dime. A quarter contains .18 of an ounce of silver and would be worth $9.00. A Walking Liberty half-dollar contains .366 of an ounce of silver and would be worth $18.30. A silver dollar contains .777 of an ounce of silver and would be worth $38.85 Make sense?

The next question is, how do I buy these silver coins? Actually, you can buy any dollar amount you want, but they generally sold in what is called a $1,000 face value bag. It is called a $1,000 face value bag because if you add up the face value of all the coins in that bag, they would equal $1,000. For example, a bag of Mercury Dimes contains 10,000 dimes, a $1,000 face value bag of quarters contains 4,000 quarters, and a bag of half dollars contains 2,000 half dollars. A $1,000 face value bag of any of these coins weighs 55 pounds and contains 715 ounces of silver. My recommendation for each of my clients is to put them into a $1,000 face value bag of silver. I generally like to put my clients into a mixture of dimes, quarters, and half dollars, and having 90% silver coins in a variety of denominations will easily suit every barter situation. That way you get a good mix of small and medium silver coins that you can use for barter. **Once your silver is in place, then you can start accumulating gold to preserve your wealth.**

Two More Good Reasons to Buy Gold and Silver – NAFTA and GATT

One final, but very important, comment before we conclude our discussion, and it directly relates to buying gold and silver. **The present economic condition of our country is much more critical than it was in 1980 when we saw the last run on gold.** Why? Because of NAFTA and GATT. With NAFTA (North American Free Trade Agreement) and GATT (General Agreement for Tariffs and Trade) having been put in place in the middle '90's, our economy, like a man with terminal cancer, is dying a slow, steady death. **Of course, our economy's demise was all planned by the New World Order people, those who have determined to reduce us to a third world country.** In a nutshell, what NAFTA and GATT have done is to remove tariffs on goods coming from other countries, and they have opened our borders to free trade with Mexico, Canada, and the rest of the world. The end result will be disaster.

Since NAFTA and GATT were put in place, we have lost over a million jobs, and over 3,000 businesses have either shut down or moved to Mexico or overseas. This process has accelerated dramatically since the beginning of 2001. In the first three months of 2001, we have lost an additional 330,000 jobs in this country. Why? How can a United States business compete with a company from Mexico paying their workers $4 a day, or a company in China paying their workers $.25 per hour? They can't. Businesses here are faced with a choice. Either close your doors, or pull up roots and set up shop in Mexico or China or Taiwan. You watch. **It is just a matter of time before our economy dies, and when that happens, what will you do?** Do you have anything to fall back on when that day comes? Do you have any real money in your possession? If you don't, you will be forced to take the mark of the New World Order beast, to buy, sell, or trade. And without getting into a discussion about the mark of the beast, suffice it to say that **if you expect to operate outside their cashless society or their plastic currency, you will have to have some gold and silver.** The only thing you can do is to personally prepare for the bad days ahead, **and a very critical part of that preparation is to have some real money in your possession.**

September 11 – The Damage, and Watch the Banks – The Shut Off Valve

The September 11, 2001, World Trade Center bombings opened a new chapter in American history – the chapter of terror. The whole country is gripped with fear – What will they do next? -- Where will they strike next? -- How can we deal with people who have no regard for their own lives? -- What about anthrax? -- What will happen to the U.S. economy? – What can I do to protect myself and my family in these perilous times? All these questions and many more are now troubling Americans.

The ramifications of the Trade Center bombings have been and will be enormous. **First of all, the effect on the insurance companies could be fatal.** In a matter of time, the insurance companies could collapse under the tremendous weight of the losses from the bombings, which will, in turn, collapse the economy. In a January 28, 2002 article from the New York Post, entitled Stunning Cost of 9/11, it states, "**The Sept. 11 terrorist attacks will cost the national economy an astonishing $639.3 billion – and some 2 million lost jobs,** a sober new state-funded report has found." The report, which cost $100,000, comes from the nationally recognized economic-forecasting firm with offices throughout the world, DRI-WEFA. The report goes on to say that, "The degree of damage from the Sept. 11

terrorist attacks on the World Trade Center is unprecedented in the United States.

Right after the bombings the airline industry cut over 100,000 jobs. Over two-thirds of their planes were mothballed in the Mojave Desert. According to the Wall Street Journal, Oct. 24, 2001, "Airline revenue collapsed by 45% in September as passenger traffic dropped 32%." The nation has been crippled in the wake of the bombings, and the worst is yet to come.

A Far More Serious Problem Is Upon Us – The Falling Dollar

More lethal to our economy than the 911 attacks, which were orchestrated by our government to create an excuse to go into Iraq to grab the oil, has been the falling dollar. That process started about the middle of 2002, and it will continue until the dollar is completely worthless. Why? Because the government and the Fed have determined to fail it. Again, Thomas Jefferson said it best years ago, **"If you can control the currency of a nation, you can control its people."** The government along with its mouthpiece, the media, has convinced the public that there is nothing wrong with the economy, that we have turned the corner and are headed into a recovery. But the steady decline of the dollar is a planned event, and things are going south, not north. The unfortunate part is that the public will not wake up until a day after it is too late.

That reminds me of the story of the frog in the pan of water on the stove. As the heat is turned up gradually to the boiling point under the pan, the frog will not make any effort to jump out of the pan to save his life. He will actually boil to his death and not do a thing about it. Unfortunately, that is the condition of the general public in this country. Even though the signs of disaster and collapse are all around us, most people refuse to open their eyes, see what is taking place, and do something about it.

The Fed Plans to Fail the Dollar

Now that sounds rather absolute doesn't it? Listen to a true story. About a year ago in May or June, 2005, I was talking to one of my main gold coin suppliers in New York City. He told me that one evening while he was taking the subway home from work, a very well-dressed, distinguished-looking gentleman sat down next to him. They struck up a conversation about the economy and the falling dollar. The smartly-dressed man started expounding about the Fed's global economic policies, interest rates, the stock market, currency exchange rates, the rising euro, and the falling dollar. This supplier friend was taken back by the man's vast knowledge of so many things.

The man went on to explain that the Federal Reserve has a 12 member board, and that six of the 12 members have determined to drop the dollar another 20% to 30% as soon as possible. At that point in time the dollar had lost over 50% of its value. Furthermore, he explained that **if the dollar were to continue to fall at its current rate, within a year and a half to two years we could have a dollar crises where the dollar would fail and become completely worthless.** The man didn't give his name, but identified himself as an analyst who worked for the Federal Reserve Bank in New York City. Since that time in June, 2006, the dollar has lost another 10% of its value. **So, at this writing, the dollar is worth only 40 cents on the 2002 dollar.** What does that mean in practical terms? If you had $100,000 in the bank or in your IRA or in T-bills or in a CD, that $100,000 is only worth $40,000 today in actual purchasing power. And how long before it is worth nothing? Just wait and see, or do something now to turn the process around. But we will deal with that a little while later.

A Falling Dollar Benefits Big Corporations and Reduces the Trade Deficit

Why is the Fed standing by and watching the demise of the dollar? Why is it that every time Bush is asked about the falling dollar he changes the subject? Let's look at a couple articles, one from the *Wall Street Journal,* and the other from the *Financial Times.* In the May 13-14, 2006, *Wall Street Journal,* the headline reads, "U.S. Quietly Hopes Dollar's Drop Eases Trade Gap." The article explains that "the White

House is quietly acquiescing in the dollar's recent slide in hopes of narrowing the U.S. trade deficit."

Key quotes in the article reveal a rather bold look at the government's intent, "But backing currency depreciation can be tricky. **The dollar's slow slide could become a steep plunge if markets turn against it—particularly if investors fear that U.S. officials are trying to engineer a drop.**" And another quote, "**A falling currency also adds to inflationary pressure at home, a fear this is increasingly rattling financial markets.**" Farther on in the article the government's intent becomes more evident, "**Treasury Secretary John Snow and other members of President Bush's economic team see continued dollar weakness . . . as the best hope for curbing the trade deficit.**" And one last quote that sums it up, "**If we're going to get our trade deficit down to manageable proportions, it's hard to see how that could happen without a very substantial depreciation of the dollar.**" Well, there it is – just as the man on the subway said. -- the government is collapsing the dollar.

Who benefits from a falling dollar? -- huge corporations. How? A weak dollar makes their products more saleable oversees. And because the government is in bed with the big corporations, they both stand on the sidelines and watch the collapse of the dollar. The real looser, however, in this whole equation is the middle class. As the dollar erodes away and loses value, the wealth of the middle class is eroded away silently, and nobody pays any attention. It is like that frog in the boiling water.

The Consumer Price Index (CPI) Lie and the Real Inflation Rate

Here is another Big Lie –the Consumer Price Index (CPI). An article from the May 14, 2006, *Financial Times*, entitled, "Greenback Takes a Pounding Over Deficit" has some key things to say about inflation, "**Worries about inflation, which have intensified since this week's meeting of the US Federal Reserve rate-setting open market committee, also sparked sharp losses in stock markets.**"

So why are the markets so concerned about inflation? Is inflation really a concern? Is it really here, or is it just a mirage? From what our government has to say, we only have between 3% and 4% inflation. Do the big boys who run the country understand the real inflation numbers? You can be sure they do. As you may not know, the Consumer Price Index or CPI, doesn't include food, fuel, or housing. So, if you take the big three out, there is nothing left. Then what is the actual rate of inflation in this country? Over the last few years while talking to people on the phone about the CPI Index I have always told them that the actual rate of inflation in this country is between 12% and 15%. People are always shocked at my number, which by the way, I couldn't prove, but I somehow had a feel for something a little closer to reality than what the government was telling us. Let's take a look at a little real research I did on actual inflation numbers over the last three years, and then I will comment after a look at this chart.

The Commodity Charts Tell the Story

To do my research I got on the internet and did a Google search for Commodities. I found the TFC Commodity Charts. These are international charts that anyone in the world with a computer can access. To get started, I picked eight common commodities that people in the United States might consume on a day-to-day basis: **heating oil, natural gas, unleaded gas, electricity, propane, coffee, orange juice, and sugar**. Then I went back to May of 2003, and noted the price for which each was trading. Then I went to May, 2006, and noted the price. I then figured the price increase over that three year period of time and came up with a percent increase over three years. The chart tells quite a story. **The actual percent increase over three years among the eight commodities was 106.6%. That equates to 35.5% inflation per year, each year for the past three years.**

Commodities	May 2003	May 2006	% Increase Over Three Years	% Increase per year
	Units	Units		
Heating Oil	0.7	2	185	
Natural Gas	5.5	7.5	36	
Unleaded Gas	0.82	2.1	156	

Electricity	55	100	81	
Propane	50	105	110	
Coffee	68	115	69	
Orange Juice	85	150	76	
Sugar	7.5	18	140	
			Actual Inflation	**Inflation per year**
Commodities Composite Increase			106.6 %	35.5 %
All metals quotes				
Copper	0.7	3.2	357	
Aluminum	65	130	100	
Palladium	165	350	112	
Platinum	600	1250	108	
Gold	340	700	**105**	
Silver	4.6	14	**204**	
All Metals Increase			164 %	54.7 %
Gold and Silver Increase			155%	51.7 %
Stock Market Increase	8500	11200	31%	10.3 %
Stock Market from 2000	10500	11200	7%	1.20%

The numbers were taken from the TFC Historical Commodity Futures Charts

The Metals Respond to Inflation – A Save Haven for Your Money

Then I did the same thing with six metals, **copper, aluminum, palladium, platinum, gold, and silver. Their increase over the same period of time from May, 2003 to May, 2006, was 164%, or 54.7% per year.** Specifically, **gold and silver increased 155%, or 51.7% per year.** Then I took a look at the stock market. From May 2003 to May, 2006, the market increased by only 31%, or 10.3% per year. The only reason that the market appreciated that much was because of the disastrous effect of 9·11 when the market dropped to 7,600 and then started recovering from there. Wishing to factor out 9·11, I went back to the year 2000 and did a comparison. **From May, 2000, to May, 2006, the stock market only went up 7%, or 1.2% per year.** When I saw the numbers I have to say I was shocked. And the chart tells the whole story.

While the dollar has lost over 60% of its value in a little over three years, the commodities we use every day have been inflated over 106%, or 35.5% a year, not 3% to 4% as the government's cooked number indicates. Specifically, then, gold and silver have gone up 155% over the past three years. Gold went from $340 per oz. in May of 2003 to $730 an oz. in April, 2006, and silver went from $4.60 per oz. in May of 2003 to $14.10 in April of 2006. If you are concerned that inflation and the falling dollar are eating up your life's savings you should take a good hard look at gold and silver.

As the Dollar Falls the Euro Rises

As the dollar continues to fall everywhere in the world, the euro is rising as the premier world currency. In fact, the American news media will never tell us this, but our dollar has been rejected in every country in the world. Every country, even Third World countries demand that we turn our dollars into euros and pay our bills. This process of converting dollars to euros has been going on around the world for over a year. That is one of the biggest reasons gold has been climbing so fast. There is no confidence in the dollar anymore. Nations like Brazil, Russia, India, and China (the BRIC Nations), have been buying gold with worthless dollars and taking physical possession of the metal. That is why gold climbed to over $700 an oz. in such a short time.

Other Dangers Ahead – Industry Collapse – War With Iran

But what will happen to the financial world in the near future? What will happen to the stock market? What will happen to the banks? What will happen when our manufacturing giants like GM, Ford, Chrysler, Delphi, IBM and many others collapse? At this writing GM, the largest manufacturer in the world, is on the verge of bankruptcy. In addition, George Bush is threatening to nuke Iran for producing nuclear weapons. If we go into Iran as we went into Iraq, we will have World War III the next day. The rest of the world is not going to sit back and watch as we slaughter thousands of innocent people just to grab someone else's oil in the name of nuclear weapons. For the past two years France and Germany have been building up armaments to come against us if we make another aggressive move. And they won't be alone. Russia and China are waiting in the wings to join them the day we set foot in Iran or pull the first trigger. And if those nations combine their military power to come against us, we don't stand a chance. What will happen to the price of gold and silver if we go into Iran? I don't really want to think about it.

The Government is Ready with Their Solution

If any or some of these things happen in the near future what about my investments and the money I have in various institutions? Are they safe? If something catastrophic happens will I be able to get my money out of harm's way in time? In 1961, Robert Anderson, the Secretary of the Treasury, drafted a document entitled the Emergency Banking Order which spells out in detail what the Federal Reserve Banking system plans to do with your money in the event of a war against the United States. They will simply close their doors and ration money to you as you need it to pay bills or taxes or for essential living expenses. But you will not be allowed to move any large amounts of money for anything. So if and when they put that order in place, forget about getting any of your money out of harm's way. The same thing is true of any of your investments, whether they are stocks, bonds, T-bills, CD's, annuities, life insurance policies, mutual funds, money market accounts. In order to cash out any of these things they need to go through a bank. And if the banks are shut down, forget it. You will never see your money again.

A wise person will see disaster coming and take steps to avoid it. Look at what happened to Argentina. With the collapse of the peso, the banks rationed cash at the rate of $250 per week or $1,000 a month. People with fortunes in the banks or in other financial institutions were stuck. Nowhere to go and nothing they can do. And with the ripple effect in motion, the question is only "When?" will it get here?

Now is the time to get your investments out of harm's way and convert them into something tangible, whether it is a stockpile of food, a wood stove, a generator, gold and silver, or cash in hand. Right now, most Americans have the majority of their electronic or paper wealth behind someone else's financial institution doors. Those investments are simply a number on a piece of paper or a number on a computer chip. It is like a digital mirage which can vaporize in an instant. But the worst and scariest part is that someone else is controlling your wealth, you are not. But the bottom line is that you are currently in control of your investments and can do something about these things if you want to. Choose your own destiny. Don't be the next victim when the banks shut their doors.

How Are You Protecting Your Financial Future?

In summation, gold has been money for over 5,000 years, being the world's only monetary metal. Gold is not just another investment – it is your family's future financial security. Don't be caught without it, and don't trade it away for anything.

****

RECOMMENDED RESOURCES:

American Numismatic Association
http://www.money.org/Content/NavigationMenu/ExploretheWorldofMoney/BuyingGold/default.htm

Federal Trade Commission
http://ftc.gov/bcp/edu/pubs/consumer/alerts/alt188.shtm

RECOMMENDED DEALERS

After a great deal of research, the author has found this dealer to be of supreme value and ethics:

California Numismatic Investments
Dealers in Precious Metals and PCGS Rare Coins
525 West Manchester Blvd.
Inglewood, CA. 90301-1627
1-800-225-7531 8:30 AM - 5:00 PM PST Monday - Friday
24-Hour Toll Free Recorded Market Report 1-888-443-4653
E-mail: info@golddealer.com, Fax 1-310-330-3766
Showroom Open: 9:00 AM - 4:30 PM PST Monday - Friday
http://www.golddealer.com/

I have personally purchased gold and silver from this dealer and visited their showroom and can vouch for their integrity.

INDEX

Australia, 12, 21, 27, 29
Bank Storage, 18
Bullion, 1, 15, 36, 41, 43, 44, 46, 48, 50, 51, 53, 55, 57, 59, 60, 88, 90, 91
Bullion Coins, 1, 41, 43, 44, 50, 51, 53, 55, 60
Bullionvault, 36
Canada, 12, 21, 133
Collectors, 63, 64
E-Bay, 14, 40
ETFs, 12, 22, 23, 24, 29
FUNDS, 19, 22
Futures, 25, 26, 51, 53, 139
Gold, 1, 2, 1, 2, 6, 9, 10, 11, 12, 13, 14, 15, 16, 17, 19, 21, 22, 23, 25, 26, 27, 28, 29, 30, 31, 32, 33, 34, 35, 36, 37, 38, 39, 40, 41, 42, 43, 44, 45, 49, 50, 51, 53, 55, 59, 60, 63, 64, 65, 67, 68, 69, 72, 73, 78, 82, 85, 86, 87, 88, 89, 91, 92, 93, 95, 96, 98, 99, 100, 103, 104, 105, 106, 107, 110, 112, 113, 122, 124, 125, 128, 130, 131, 133, 139, 140, 142
GOLD, 6, 9, 12, 14, 17, 29, 32, 37
GOLDMONEY, 34
Great Britain, 5
inflation, 3, 4, 5, 7, 9, 33, 50, 86, 96, 99, 102, 112, 131, 137, 138, 140
interest rates, 3, 5, 6, 69, 85, 99, 131, 135
Internet, 1, 30, 37, 40, 66, 67
Investing, 1, 21, 24, 38, 42, 50, 53, 55, 56, 60
MINING, 19
Nigeria, 39
Paypal, 31, 33, 40
Perth Mint, 27, 28, 29, 34
precious metals, 2, 12, 16, 17, 29, 33, 37, 40, 41, 43, 45, 46, 51, 59, 61, 65, 66, 88, 93, 94, 95, 128, 130
Reference, 1, 48
Silver, 1, 2, 1, 2, 7, 11, 12, 13, 15, 16, 17, 22, 23, 24, 26, 28, 30, 31, 33, 35, 36, 37, 41, 43, 44, 78, 89, 95, 99, 130, 132, 133, 139
SILVER, 6, 12, 14, 17, 29, 37
South Africa, 12, 21, 87

SPREAD BETTING, 24
Stock Market, 20, 120, 139
Zimbabwe, 5

www.ingramcontent.com/pod-product-compliance
Lightning Source LLC
Chambersburg PA
CBHW030940090426
42737CB00007B/486